D0161987

North Africa in Transition
The Struggle for Democracies and Institutions

Edited by Ben Fishman

North Africa in Transition
The Struggle for Democracies and Institutions

Edited by Ben Fishman

IISS The International Institute for Strategic Studies

The International Institute for Strategic Studies

Arundel House | 13–15 Arundel Street | Temple Place | London | WC2R 3DX | UK

First published November 2015 **Routledge**
4 Park Square, Milton Park, Abingdon, Oxon, OX14 4RN

for **The International Institute for Strategic Studies**
Arundel House, 13–15 Arundel Street, Temple Place, London, WC2R 3DX, UK
www.iiss.org

Simultaneously published in the USA and Canada by **Routledge**
270 Madison Ave., New York, NY 10016

Routledge is an imprint of Taylor & Francis, an Informa Business

© 2015 The International Institute for Strategic Studies

DIRECTOR-GENERAL AND CHIEF EXECUTIVE Dr John Chipman
EDITOR Dr Nicholas Redman
EDITORIAL MANAGER Nancy Turner
ASSISTANT EDITOR Mona Moussavi
EDITORIAL Bonnie Bley, James Middleton
COVER/PRODUCTION John Buck, Kelly Verity
COVER IMAGES Getty/EPA

The International Institute for Strategic Studies is an independent centre for research, information and debate on the problems of conflict, however caused, that have, or potentially have, an important military content. The Council and Staff of the Institute are international and its membership is drawn from almost 100 countries. The Institute is independent and it alone decides what activities to conduct. It owes no allegiance to any government, any group of governments or any political or other organisation. The IISS stresses rigorous research with a forward-looking policy orientation and places particular emphasis on bringing new perspectives to the strategic debate.

The Institute's publications are designed to meet the needs of a wider audience than its own membership and are available on subscription, by mail order and in good book-shops. Further details at www.iiss.org.

Printed and bound in Great Britain by Bell & Bain Ltd, Thornliebank, Glasgow

All rights reserved. No part of this book may be reprinted or reproduced or utilised in any form or by any electronic, mechanical, or other means, now known or hereaf-ter invented, including photocopying and recording, or in any information storage or retrieval system, without permission in writing from the publishers.

British Library Cataloguing in Publication Data
A catalogue record for this book is available from the British Library

Library of Congress Cataloging in Publication Data

ADELPHI series
ISSN 1944-5571

ADELPHI 452
ISBN 978-1-138-65335-1

Contents

	Contributors	6
Introduction	**North Africa in Transition** Ben Fishman	9
Chapter One	**Tunisia: Foundations of Democratic Compromise** Nicole Rowsell	19
Chapter Two	**Libya: From Euphoria to Breakdown** Borzou Daragahi	39
Chapter Three	**Power and Authority in Morocco** Haim Malka	59
Chapter Four	**Algeria: Enter the Oligarchy** Geoff D. Porter	79
Chapter Five	**Jihadism in North Africa: A House of Many Mansions** Jean-Pierre Filiu	97
Chapter Six	**A New Economic Model for North Africa** Svetlana Milbert	113
Conclusion	**The Challenges on Implementing Institutional Reform** Ben Fishman	131
	Index	151

Borzou Daragahi, a three-time Pulitzer finalist, is a Middle East correspondent at BuzzFeed News, based in Istanbul. He has been covering the Middle East and North Africa since 2002, spending a significant amount of time in Libya for the *Los Angeles Times* and *Financial Times*.

Jean-Pierre Filiu is a professor of Middle East Studies at Sciences Po and served as a career diplomat from 1988–2006. He is the author of several books, most recently *From Deep State to Islamic State: the Arab Counter-Revolution and its Jihadi Legacy* (Oxford, 2015).

Ben Fishman is a consulting senior fellow for the Middle East and North Africa at the International Institute for Strategic Studies. He served on the US National Security Council from 2009–2013, where his responsibilities included North Africa.

Haim Malka is a senior fellow and deputy director of the Middle East Program at the Center for Strategic and International Studies, where he oversees the program's work on the Maghreb.

Svetlana Milbert is an economist focused on the Middle East and North Africa. From 2012–2014, she was assistant director for economic research at the Rafik Hariri Center for the Middle East at the Atlantic Council.

Geoff D. Porter is an Assistant Professor at the Combating Terrorism Center at West Point, and the founder of North Africa Risk Consulting, Inc., a consulting firm specialising in political and security risk in North Africa.

Nicole Rowsell oversaw the establishment of the National Democratic Institute (NDI)'s office in Tunisia in 2011, where the Institute worked to help nascent political parties, candidates and citizen-monitoring organisations prepare for the country's first democratic elections. She is currently NDI's resident director in Lebanon.

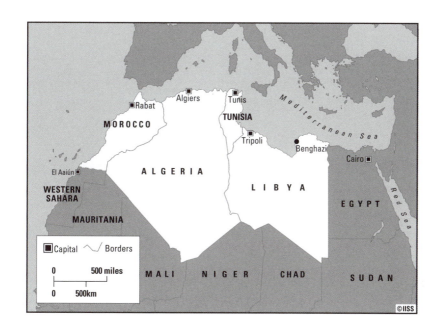

North Africa in Transition

For well over a generation, continuity was the watchword for the four countries at the heart of North Africa – Morocco, Algeria, Tunisia and Libya. Politics did not vary much following the end of French colonial rule in Morocco and Tunisia in the 1950s or Algerian independence in 1962, despite the occasional handover of leadership. Muammar Gadhafi grabbed international headlines for sponsoring terrorism, but the brutal and bizarre Jamahiriya he created and led for 42 years drew far less attention. Algeria's 1991 election opened debates about the popular appeal of Islamist movements, but that debate would have to wait 20 years after the regime cancelled the election, provoking a horrific civil war and giving birth to some of the region's earliest jihadist groups.

Absent dramatic political change in the region, scholars sought to explain authoritarian resilience and why the Middle East and North Africa had managed to withstand the 'waves' of democratisation that had prevailed in Asia, Latin America, Eastern Europe and much of Africa. They pointed to the police states of these regimes, the loyalty and effectiveness of security services, the persistent disorganisation of opposition groups and oil wealth for those regimes that benefitted from it. One scholar explained the success of regimes in resisting democratic trends as 'upgrading authoritarianism': allowing cosmetic alterations, such as having nominal elections or controlled market liberalisation, without changing the fundamental power structures.[1] In other words, most experts dismissed the prospects of revolution in the Middle East and North Africa right up until the revolutions transpired. At a United States (US) State Department-sponsored conference in 2010 between US government officials and academic experts, no participant was willing to go out on a limb and suggest political transitions were possible – much less imminent – despite acknowledging growing youth populations and the ubiquity of new forms of social media that old methods of suppression would soon find harder to contain. The US National Security Council held a series of inter-agency discussions in 2010 and was drafting a presidential directive that would have elevated issues of political and economic reform in our bilateral relations with Middle East governments, when the Arab uprisings surprised everyone.[2]

The popular unrest that started in Tunisia in late 2010 and spread across North Africa and the wider Middle East happened at a pace no one predicted. Within a matter of months, decades-old regimes and their leaders were gone: Zine al-Abidine Ben Ali in Tunisia; Gadhafi in Libya; Ali Abdullah Saleh in Yemen; and most dramatically, Hosni Mubarak in Egypt. Monarchies in Morocco, Jordan and Bahrain enacted reforms to varying degrees in attempts to stave off wider-scale protests. Tragically, Syria descended into a vicious civil war.

Scholars of the Middle East have begun to examine why they failed to predict the Arab Spring and to identify root causes of the uprisings.[3] They have focused on the organisational tactics of protesters, new methods of exploiting social media and the commitment of security forces to defending now-vulnerable regimes.[4] Foreign intelligence agencies have also recognised, in hindsight, that they relied too heavily on what their counterparts said was happening inside their own countries rather than developing their own sources within a host nation.

Few authors, however, have analysed the Middle East's sub-regions to assess how the uprisings emerged and the distinct ways in which they have developed since the drama of 2011. This book begins the conversation where the uprisings originated, examining why revolutions transpired in Tunisia and Libya but not in Morocco or Algeria.

A distinct grouping

The Maghreb (literally, west or the western Arab world, as opposed to the Mashreq, encompassing Egypt, the Levant and the Gulf to the east) has distinct cultural, ethnic, geographic, religious and historical experiences that are worth studying. The countries of this sub-region, for example, all share a Mediterranean coastline and proximity to Europe, as opposed to the vast deserts interrupted by the Nile, Tigris and Euphrates Vallies – the 'fertile crescent' around which much of Arab civilisation emerged. Foreign conquerors, whether the Caliphate from Damascus or the Ottomans, gave the Maghreb relatively more independence given its distance and comparative value to Egypt, the Levant, or the Hejaz. Egypt, in contrast, has always considered itself central to the Arab world, the country that has the longest history of self-government, and therefore an almost innate sense of nationalism.

Not until the 19th century did Europe, specifically France, begin to view the Maghreb as an essential part of its colonial enterprise.

French colonial rule began in Algeria in the early 19th century and later extended to Morocco and Tunisia, though Algeria was an actual colony while the other two were protectorates, with somewhat more authority granted to local leaders. France had several years – and in Algeria's case, decades – to modernise the territories in question and establish the early vestiges of local bureaucracy. As historian Michael Willis describes, 'whatever political authority succeeded colonial control at independence would inherit a highly efficient, highly centralized and thus highly powerful state apparatus.'[5] In contrast, British influence in the region (throughout most of the Mashreq after the First World War) was shorter in duration and more contested by nationalist forces. Libya stands apart as the only country in the Middle East that experienced Italian colonial rule, followed by an 18-year monarchy, before Gadhafi's coup. Even within Libya, there are significant differences between east, west and south, dating back well before pre-modern times (famously, Libyans in the west eat couscous and rice in the east).

Although the region is predominantly Arab, minority groups include ethnic Berbers, Touareg and other tribally based societies that extend beyond the region's formal borders and into less-governed territory. Governments have tended to focus their attention on the coastal cities, ignoring the interior regions, which has caused increasing economic and security problems across the region. These include the rise in smuggling and human-trafficking, ungoverned spaces exploited by terrorists, and economic disparity that has led to anti-government protests, including oil strikes. Indeed, the first major protest that launched the Arab uprisings was the self-immolation of a fruit vendor in the Tunisian interior town of Sidi Bouzid.

The vast majority of North Africa is Sunni Muslim, but unlike the rest of the Middle East, the dominant religious influences stem from the Maliki school of jurisprudence and the spiritual influence of Sufism, with its rituals and respect for Muslim 'saints' (distinct from the puritanical Wahhabism dominant in the Gulf). In fact, as extremist Islam has spread across North Africa, a common target of attacks has been Sufi shrines.

Why exclude Egypt? The answer is both substantive and pragmatic. Firstly, the size, scope and complexity of Egypt make it especially challenging to capture in one relatively brief chapter. The International Institute for Strategic Studies will therefore devote a separate volume entirely to the country. Secondly, while many comparisons can be drawn between the long-time rules of Mubarak and Gadhafi, Abdelaziz Bouteflika, Ben Ali and even King Mohammed VI, Egypt was never resource-rich (unlike Algeria and Libya) and Mubarak derived much of his legitimacy in the West from his proximity to and role in the Israel-Palestine conflict. Egypt is clearly a major player in the politics and security of North Africa but would overwhelm a single study of the region.

Similarly, Mauritania is excluded from this study, although it is technically a member of the Arab League (and the barely active Arab Maghreb Union). Mauritania is arguably closer in ethnic and demographic composition and recent political history to its Malian and Nigerien neighbours in the Sahel than to the states of North Africa. Western Sahara, the disputed territory between Morocco and Algeria, is also excluded. Rival claims by the parties appear to have not been significantly affected by the 2011 uprisings and are no closer to resolution than when the United Nations (UN) established a peacekeeping force there in 1989.

Political change in its regional context

The factors mentioned earlier – colonial legacy, ethnic diversity and ungoverned spaces – long predated the dramatic upheavals in 2011 and thus explain little about the origins of the uprisings. In fact, scholarship of North Africa has featured few comparative studies of the sub-region, perhaps because little had changed in recent decades – with the notable exception of Algeria's brutal civil war.[6]

Today's circumstances, however, are radically different. Tunisia and Libya have attracted attention from journalists, researchers and democracy practitioners since the overthrow of Ben Ali and Gadhafi, as well as the divergent paths taken since their initial revolutions. But Morocco and Algeria deserve just as much focus for the revolutions that might have been but failed to materialise. Not including these stories when reviewing the uprisings in North Africa risks telling an incomplete story of the drivers of political change and the response of all four countries to enormous pressure for reform.

This book argues that North Africa represents a microcosm of what the broader Middle East experienced and thus offers lessons for the entire region. It tells the story of how four neighbouring countries responded in distinct ways to the most dramatic political change in the Arab world in at least a generation: Tunisia, with its hitherto largely successful democratic transition; Libya, with its popular revolution but inability to transform newly earned individual freedoms into national unity, leading to a breakdown of political order and civil war; Morocco, with its palace-led political reforms that purport to devolve power from the king to an elected government; and Algeria, with its use of state wealth to stave off potential political unrest. The book also addresses several underlying challenges in the region that endure (and perhaps have been aggravated) despite political change, namely economic grievances and the growing jihadist threat, which now includes the pan-regional Islamic State of Iraq and al-Sham (ISIS), as well as localised groups, such as Ansar al-Sharia and al-Mourabitoun.

In all these cases, all segments of government desperately need institutional reform. While all four countries suffered from economic inequality and a lack of opportunities to pursue individual dignity, the institutional deficits in Libya and Tunisia were particularly severe, with the arbitrariness of Gadhafi's regime and the crony capitalism under Ben Ali. In contrast, Morocco and Algeria had just enough institutional legitimacy (from the former's monarchy and the latter's elite *pouvoir*) to enable them to make important policy decisions in the early months of 2011 that withstood the regional tide of unrest.

North African states need to learn how to provide security and respect the rule of law, while distancing themselves from the practices of brutal police states. To respond to citizens' demands for dignity and opportunity, governments must adopt economic reforms that promote job creation and private-sector growth – steps that may often be challenged by the entrenched interests of the elite, and youth populations who have grown accustomed to public-sector employment and subsidies for everyday goods. In sum, whatever form of government exists, modernising political, economic and security institutions with the aim of improving transparency and accountability will enable North African citizens to feel more invested in the future of their governments. In turn, this will make them less inclined to launch sustained protests or follow a path toward radicalisation. Assisting the design, implementation and communication of such reforms should be a key function of the West's engagement with the region.

By examining the experiences of each of these North African countries, the book not only seeks to analyse developments in the region but also to draw attention to potential lessons for the wider Arab world: how and where can Islamists and secular or non-Islamist parties coexist (is Tunisia unique or can Egypt or Fatah and Hamas emulate the Tunisian model)? Why did the Libyan state break down so quickly after the revolution and what could it reveal about Syria after its civil war? How far do reforms need to go to preserve stability in Morocco and what can monarchies such as Jordan learn from its example? Finally, how long can hydrocarbon-rich states in the Middle East afford to avoid democratisation? While this *Adelphi* focuses on North Africa, it should be read with these broader questions in mind.

Western interests

The US and Europe need to better understand and invest in North Africa if they are going to manage the growing terrorism and migration crises emanating from the southern Mediterranean. Not since the early 1960s has the region played a more significant role in Europe's interests and stability. Two tragic examples illustrate this point.

Firstly, on 16 January 2013, al-Qaeda-linked militants attacked the In Amenas gas plant in southern Algeria, operated jointly between Norway's Statoil and BP, taking more than 100 foreigners hostage and sparking a stand-off that lasted three days. When the hostage-takers attempted to escape, Algerian security forces launched a heavy-handed response, leaving 39 foreigners dead, including five Britons, five Norwegians, ten Japanese and three US citizens. It became all too evident that despite extensive energy-sector links between Europe and North Africa, ties at the political and security levels were extremely limited, especially with the Algerians who are highly suspicious of anything resembling foreign intervention. That dynamic improved slightly in 2013, when Algeria opened its airspace to French warplanes and US refuelling tankers conducting operations in northern Mali. However, it still has a long way to go to reach more consistent security cooperation, both internally within North Africa and beyond.

Secondly, on 26 June 2015, a lone gunman with links to the Islamic State killed 38, mostly British, tourists on a beach resort in Sousse, Tunisia. It was the deadliest terrorist attack on British citizens since the July 2005 bombings in London. Despite the impressive progress Tunisia has made, the only Arab democracy is still suffering from substantial security and economic challenges that it will have to overcome to secure its democratic future. As the popularity of ISIS increases across the Middle East and among disaffected Muslims in Europe, securing closer government-to-government ties with North Africa will be required to address the interconnected problems of terrorism, extremism, migration and economic stability.

In the years ahead, Europe will become more deeply enmeshed in North African affairs. The migration crisis, which has complicated roots in sub-Saharan Africa, exacerbated by instability in Libya, Egypt and Syria, has increasingly involved the European Union (EU). Several member states now contribute naval assets under the Italian-led *Operation Triton*, interdicting illegal smuggling craft and often forced to rescue migrants aboard. The European Council released a broader strategy to confront the migration crisis in May 2015.[7] In Libya, the US, EU, United Kingdom (UK), France, Germany, Italy and Spain backed months-long UN-led negotiations to forge the National Unity Agreement. As the Government of National Accord seeks to establish some credibility with the Libyan population, enhance security and confront terrorism, its international partners have pledged support. This will potentially include some form of a stabilisation force to protect government institutions and train Libyan security forces, drawing Europe back into the region militarily in a way it has not been since French forces withdrew from Algeria more than 50 years ago.

In sum, North Africa's problems can no longer be contained in North Africa. This book attempts to better inform readers and policymakers about the key political, economic and security challenges facing this under-studied region. It is an analysis of how North Africa emerged after the Arab uprisings and why four countries – Morocco, Algeria, Tunisia and Libya – have undertaken very different trajectories.

Notes

1 Steven Heydemann, 'Upgrading Authoritarianism in the Arab World', Center for Middle East Policy Analysis Papers, no. 13, October 2007. See also, Larry Diamond, 'Why Are There No Arab Democracies?', *Journal of Democracy*, vol. 21, no. 1, January 2010, pp. 93–104; and Daniel Brumberg, 'The Trap of Liberalized Autocracy', *Journal of Democracy*, vol. 13, no. 4, October 2002, pp. 56–68.

2 Ryan Lizza, 'The Consequentialist: How the Arab Spring Remade Obama's Foreign Policy', *The New Yorker*, May 2, 2011. The author participated in these discussions.

3 F. Gregory Gause, 'Why Middle East Studies Missed the Arab Spring: The Myth of Arab Authoritarianism', *Foreign Affairs*, vol. 90, no. 4, July/August 2011, http://www.foreignaffairs.com/articles/67932/f-gregory-gause-iii/why-middle-east-studies-missed-the-arab-spring.

4 Marc Lynch, *The Arab Uprising: The Unfinished Revolutions of the New Middle East* (New York: Public Affairs, 2012); and Eva Bellin, 'Reconsidering the Robustness of Authoritarianism in the Middle East: Lessons from the Arab Spring', *Comparative Politics*, vol. 44, no. 2, 2012, pp. 127–49.

5 Michael J. Willis, *Politics and Power in the Maghreb: Algeria, Tunisia and Morocco from Independence to the Arab Spring* (Oxford: Oxford University Press, 2014), p. 34.

6 One notable exception is Willis' recent comparative study of Algeria, Morocco and Tunisia prior to the Arab uprisings, which excludes Libya. Other exceptions include: Dirk Vandewalle (ed.), *North Africa: Development and Reform in a Changing Global Economy* (New York: St. Martin's Press, 1996); and Anthony H. Cordesman, *A Tragedy of Arms: Military and Security Developments in the Maghreb* (Westport, CT: Praeger, 2002).

7 European Commission, 'Communication From The Commission To The European Parliament, The Council, The European Economic And Social Committee And The Committee Of The Regions A European Agenda On Migration', Brussels, 13 May 2015, http://ec.europa.eu/dgs/home-affairs/what-we-do/policies/european-agenda-migration/background-information/docs/communication_on_the_european_agenda_on_migration_en.pdf.

CHAPTER ONE

Tunisia: Foundations of Democratic Compromise

Nicole Rowsell

Prior to the protests that began in the winter of 2010, the conventional wisdom on Tunisia held that many citizens would tolerate the country's closed political system in exchange for economic benefits and stability. However, this bargain became increasingly unsustainable; a global economic crisis, along with corruption and favouritism under then-president Zine al-Abidine Ben Ali, contributed to a disturbingly high unemployment rate among Tunisia's well-educated youth. Calls for dignity – driven by unmet economic, social and political needs – toppled Tunisia's one-party system, which had dominated the country in the decades since independence from France.

The aspirations of Tunisians inspired citizens across the Middle East and North Africa to call for similar change. In the years since these uprisings in several Arab countries, Tunisia remains the best – and perhaps only – case where those calls for change have contributed to positive political reform. Undoubtedly, political gains have been hard fought, and Tunisia's transition remains fragile as newly acquired democratic values must take root amid very real threats. While Tunisia's success to date is based on a number of unique underlying factors, its democratic transition does offer insights that could resonate well beyond Tunisia's borders.

The foundations of Tunisia's transition

As the birthplace of the Arab uprisings, Tunisia's transition has been supported by several factors. A small country with a relatively homogenous population and limited experience of division along ethnic or religious lines, Tunisian societal patterns were reinforced by Ottoman and then French colonial powers who viewed the region as a hinterland of sorts. The period of 380 years of colonial rule in Tunisia was relatively lenient compared to the treatment received by other parts of the empires; nonetheless, it definitively shaped the political and administrative frameworks the country inherited.

In particular, the legal and financial systems imported by the French laid the foundation for a dominant state apparatus, which centralised power in the capital and eroded autonomy in rural areas, where prominent families had previously exercised greater control. Improvements in infrastructure, including building a road network throughout the country and making basic education available, helped strengthen allegiance to the central administration in Tunis.

It was during Tunisia's period as a protectorate under French rule that the seeds of constitutional rule and party-based politics were planted. In 1920, the Destour (constitution in Arabic) party was established, calling for a constitutional process that would open the door for a parliament to create accountable governance. Habib Bourguiba rose up within the party and eventually became the leader of its reformed neo-Destour platform, which prioritised independence from France. Through savvy negotiations with the French that leveraged an important alliance with the leading trade union,[1] while stamping out internal conflicts within his own party,

Bourguiba positioned himself to become the country's first post-independence president and overseer of Tunisia's first constitution-drafting process. Through an elected constituent assembly, the two-year process, which concluded in 1959, and consisted of negotiating articles of the constitution, outlined a central role for the presidency and provided for the creation of a supporting parliament.[2]

This centralisation of power – often linked as much to the personality, as the prerogatives, of the president – over time made the office vulnerable. Bourguiba's vision to modernise the Tunisian state and society was contingent on dominance of his political party over the vestiges of secular state power. Over time, the structures of the party were reformed to reflect the hierarchy of local and regional administrations, ensuring the party was pervasive in the daily life of Tunisians.[3]

Bourguiba's influence also extended to the role of the military in Tunisian society. Driven by his desire for complete loyalty and concerned that some early attempts to unseat him had come from within army ranks, Bourguiba worked to sever the military from political institutions. With civilian leadership and a ban on political participation (party membership and voting rights were forbidden by law), Tunisia's military assumed a subservient role to the executive, which it largely maintained throughout the following 60 years.

Nevertheless, the size and power of the military expanded. The most notable evidence of this was Bourguiba's removal from office by a former military official, Zine al-Abidine Ben Ali, in 1987. Following the overthrow of Tunisia's first post-independence president, Ben Ali set about consolidating power in his own name, as Bourguiba had before him, keeping the military at a distance and instead relying on intelligence-gathering and detentions by separate security units within the Ministry of Interior.

While Ben Ali's 23-year rule was characterised by further investments in infrastructure and the allowance of a limited number of opposition political parties, these moves were ultimately cosmetic and focused on benefitting his immediate circle of family and friends. The increasing level of opulence demonstrated by regime-linked individuals and businesses steadily built public resentment; first lady Leila Ben Ali's extravagant spending and her extended family's virtual monopoly over entire industries, including hotels and insurance, garnered the most vocal criticism. This political and social marginalisation of the population, coupled with a failed economic development model driven by socialist and protectionist policies, and deep-seated corruption, created a brittle system vulnerable to growing citizen frustrations. Mohamed Bouazizi's self-immolation on the steps of a government building in the central town of Sidi Bouzid in December 2010 not only demonstrated this sense of despair and resonated with the population, but then also served as a catalyst for popular protests propelled by the widespread use of social media. Ben Ali responded with a mixture of force (the transitional government estimated at least 300 protesters had been killed during the protests) and half-hearted pledges to meet the demands of protesters. Eventually though, he conceded and fled the country in January, less than a month after the first protests.[4] The fact that several members of the extended first family chose to flee the country in response to the growing protests demonstrated a profound disconnect from the realities of average Tunisians.

Initial optimism

After Ben Ali's ousting, Tunisians were extremely optimistic about their prospects; they had high expectations that newly elected authorities could deliver greater economic opportunity, respect for the rule of law and better services in healthcare and education. In public-opinion research conducted by the National Democratic Institute (NDI) following the October 2011 elections, Tunisian respondents outlined clear objectives for the incoming National Constituent Assembly (NCA) and political leadership:

> Tunisians expect political leaders to immediately address the economic stagnation that has gripped the country since the revolution...participants hold interim government officials responsible for resolving the country's economic crisis, and expect newly elected representatives to develop policies and plans in the next year.
>
> Participants consistently mention the need for a change in mentality to address the pervasive sense of victimhood that was perpetuated under the Ben Ali regime. Confronting the legacy of the previous regime and holding individuals accountable are seen as benchmarks for measuring political progress and rebuilding the sense of social unity.
>
> Safeguarding pluralist, inclusive, accountable decision-making through citizen vigilance is viewed as a political and security imperative... Citizens generally link timely political progress to enhanced security.
>
> Reform of public administration will be required to build more responsive institutions – another key benchmark in determining democratic progress. Participants specifically list healthcare, education, agricultural production and transport and service industries as areas requiring reform.[5]

But as with all transitional governments, the interim authorities and the NCA struggled to meet these expectations. In the first years after the revolution, politics subsumed policy, even as technical elements of the transition mostly proceeded peacefully.

Accomplishments

Revisiting the constituent assembly model

When Ben Ali and his extended family fled the country, the set of institutions he had led largely remained intact. While some basic services, from garbage collection to policing, ceased in the immediate aftermath, the consistent presence of the army, in an attempt to maintain public order, helped reassure the population. This allowed critical time for political leaders to develop a plan for the next steps of the transition. The legacy of Tunisian bureaucracy, dating back to the French mandate, served a positive function at this delicate time, because public servants, keen to maintain the relative job security of the public sector, were willing to return to work, even in the face of questions about political leadership. In the proceeding weeks, as an interim government led by members of the former regime tried to assert control, the public repeatedly took to the streets, ultimately forcing two holdover governments to resign, under the watchful eye of military leaders who refrained from intervening in the political process. In early March, Béji Caïd Essebsi, an experienced Tunisian politician who had credentials as a Ben Ali critic, assumed the role of interim prime minister. Transitional governance bodies, anointed by Ben Ali, adapted to make key political decisions about the transition that required ratification by Essebsi's government and put in place an electoral framework. The High Commission for the Fulfillment of the Goals of the Revolution, Political Reform and Democratic Transition – one of three such bodies created in the final days of Ben Ali's rule – was expanded from a small committee of technical experts to a larger, and more inclusive, political body comprising civic activists and representatives from leading political parties.

These leaders were able to proceed relatively quickly, with public support, given their chosen model for the transition: the establishment of a constituent assembly to revise Tunisia's constitution, and only then holding national elections. A similar model had been employed, following independence from the French, to draft the country's first constitution and facilitate the handover to a new government. Elections in October 2011 for the NCA essentially focused the debate in Tunis on the contours of a future political system, including separation of powers and the extent to which rights and freedoms would be respected and protected by the constitution. By prioritising negotiations for the political framework, parties that wanted to govern were forced to first compromise on a system of checks and balances, which would ultimately diffuse decision-making across branches of government.

Developing an inclusive electoral framework

The NCA elections marked a critical step in Tunisia's transition to democracy. They were widely considered to be inclusive, competitive and successful, with the results accepted by most stakeholders, despite technical weaknesses. The temporary election administration, the Instance Supérieure Indépendante pour les Élections (ISIE), won high praise for its independence, commitment and honesty, as well as its ability to deliver successful elections under the pressure of a short timeframe and difficult circumstances.

After years of tight control, the Tunisian political arena blossomed throughout 2011. More than 100 political parties were licensed and submitted candidate lists, alongside scores of independents who wished to compete for seats in the NCA elections. These political parties varied in ideology and experience. Ennahda – a previously banned political movement, with an Islamist ideology – surged in popularity, due as much to its disciplined, grassroots outreach, highlighting its symbolism of struggle against the previous regime. Its leader, the previously exiled Sheikh Rached Ghannouchi, trumpeted the view that Islam was compatible with democracy. Conversely, secular parties proliferated but struggled to define concrete platforms and differentiate themselves in the eyes of first-time voters.

In total, 1,662 candidate lists competed in the 33 electoral districts representing Tunisians living in the country, as well as key constituencies abroad. Continuing the country's heritage of progressive legislation towards women, all competing lists required alternation between male and female candidates, also referred to as a 'zipper system'. These groups faced similar challenges as they sought to overcome inexperience, a nebulous legal framework and entrenched suspicions of political organising.

By the same token, civil-society organisations with diverse aims and constituencies proliferated throughout Tunisia, many of whom were citizen monitors during the NCA elections. For the first time in history, more than 10,000 citizens had organised themselves to scrutinise election-day operations, including voting and counting procedures.

Exploring coalition politics

The results of the NCA elections – with 27 party, independent and coalition lists winning seats – were a shock to smaller parties, which had focused limited resources on grassroots election-campaigning and therefore did not fare as well as they had hoped. Although no party won a majority of seats, Ennahda emerged as the strongest political force in the country, securing five times the popular vote of the runner-up. Drawing on a nationwide base that had suffered repression under Ben

Ali, Ennahda emerged from the 2011 elections not only with the strongest brand but also with the most confidence from the electorate.[6] The movement's leadership – both those who returned from exile and those released from prison in the days after Ben Ali's departure – helped to fortify the image of a political institution, rather than relying on the charisma of one or two individuals, as some other parties did.

Ennahda's leadership also moved quickly after the elections to establish a power-sharing framework, along with counterparts from the Congress for the Republic (CPR) and Ettakatol, two secular parties whose election results most closely trailed Ennahda. Popularly referred to as the troika, this coalition set about dividing up key posts in the NCA and interim government between their party loyalists. However, from the outset, the coalition struggled to articulate a clear vision for managing the constitutional period, which eroded trust among the party's leadership and eventually with the public at large too.

With Ennahda's success came disappointing results for Tunisia's secular parties, many of which had attempted, but failed during the pre-election period, to form a broad-based coalition. In January 2012, five parties, most notably the Progressive Democratic Party and Afek Tounes, announced their decision to merge in order to create a centrist counterweight to the majority coalition. Later that year, former transitional prime minister Essebsi called for disparate groups of Tunisian society to come together under yet another new party, Nidaa Tounes. Claiming linkages to the Destourian movement and a track record of governance, a constellation of well-known leaders joined the party, which aimed to build its prominence on opposition to Ennahda and nostalgia for post-independence rule. The party drew controversy for including figures from the former regime, and in an attempt to appeal to a broader cross-section of potential voters, initiated negotiations with several other parties to create an electoral alliance. However, delays in drafting the constitution, punctuated by a complete stall of the NCA's work following assassinations in 2013 of two prominent secular politicians, allowed Nidaa Tounes to further build its base. It established an electoral alliance with four other secular parties, under the banner 'Union for Tunisia'.

However, coalition-building preoccupied the attention and time of political leaders, regardless of their affiliation, and further delayed the constitution-drafting process, beyond the original one-year mandate of the NCA. The government, which mainly served in an interim capacity, struggled to define and implement policies in key areas, such as economic initiatives and security, waiting for a more permanent government to take potentially controversial positions.

Public oversight of the constitutional process

Following elections, NCA deputies set about their first task of drafting internal by-laws, which would outline the constitution-drafting process and other legislative responsibilities. A loose coalition of civil-society organisations, created in spring 2011 with a common goal of improving government transparency, seized this important opportunity. It launched an advocacy campaign calling for all plenary and committee meetings to be open to the public. This transparency agenda, adopted by the NCA in its internal rules of procedure, resulted in plenary sessions being broadcast on public television and radio stations. Citizens and civil-society groups were also given access to plenary sessions, and in certain instances, the working sessions of constitutional and regular legislative committees. While the NCA leadership received criticism for not communicating its agenda and progress to the public in a consistent manner, entrepreneurial Tunisian associations still managed to establish a monitoring framework for the assembly's work. The work of watchdog organisation Al Bawsala,[7] in particular, not only provided important information to the public, but also held deputies accountable by tracking and publishing voting records, in addition to publishing decisions in real time through popular social-media platforms.

It was in part due to this close monitoring that civil-society organisations could mobilise so quickly following the release of the first draft of the constitution in August 2012. The draft drew controversy for describing women as complementary to men. In response, human-rights activists staged a series of public protests and lobbied individual deputies within the ruling coalition bloc to reconsider. The text was revised and Tunisia's adopted constitution now states that women are equal to men.

Alternative mechanisms for negotiation

Amid contentious deliberations over the constitution, the February 2013 assassination of leftist opposition figure Chokri Belaid raised political tensions and galvanised politicians to move forwards with a long-discussed cabinet reshuffle. Prime Minister Hamadi Jebali, a moderate within Ennahda, vowed to create a technocratic government but ultimately failed to convince other Ennahda leaders, especially Ghannouchi, who held sway over Ennahda's governing Shura Council. The debate within Ennahda had been building for some time, with Ghannouchi advocating a tolerant approach to the violent Salafists of Ansar al-Sharia, even after their tactics shifted from attacking stores that sold alcohol and art galleries to a brazen attack against the US Embassy on 11 September 2012. Ghannouchi believed he could persuade Ansar al-Sharia not to interfere with the political process that he hoped would yield a significant win for political Islam. But his inability to prevent the first political assassination led to a major backlash against the Ennahda-controlled government and within weeks the government banned Ansar al-Sharia from meeting. It later declared the group a terrorist organisation.

Following Jebali's resignation in February, Ennahda leaders agreed to yield key ministries to technocrats and tapped Interior Minister Ali Laarayedh, a member of Ennahda, to form a government. However, he was unable to enlarge the governing coalition and the troika remained unchanged. A second assassination of a political figure in July – this time a member of the assembly – again threatened to derail the political process; a coalition of parties, led by newcomer Nidaa Tounes and the leftist Popular Front, called for the overthrow of the Ennahda-led government and dissolution of the assembly. Troika leaders, including assembly president Mustapha Ben Jaafar, balked at these threats, making the case that if the assembly were disbanded, the country would enter into a legal vacuum with no framework for progress. While the assembly's credibility was seriously questioned after its inability to complete the constitution by the original deadline in 2012, its legitimacy as the only elected institution proved to be resilient.

After weeks of shuttle diplomacy between the key factions, a framework for negotiations emerged. A steering committee of sorts, comprising four civil-society groups, led by the prominent Tunisian General Labour Union (UGTT) and known collectively as 'the quartet', proposed a roadmap referred to as the 'National Dialogue' process. The talks, which included a series of ambitious deadlines, had four key aims: creating an apolitical government of technocrats to replace the tripartite coalition government; reaching agreement on final sticking points in the draft constitution; appointing the leadership of an independent election administration responsible for drafting the election law; and agreeing on the sequence and timing of presidential and parliamentary elections.

While agreement on a new prime minister proved difficult, the political leadership eventually agreed to hand over the cabinet to Mehdi Jomaa, who was serving in the troika government at the time as minister of industry. In late December 2013, the parties agreed that the government handover and three other processes – the adoption of the new constitution, agreement on an election date and selection of ISIE members – would be completed.

While Tunisian politicians commonly referred to the process as one of consensus-building, in fact the National Dialogue was an excellent example of facilitating political compromise to move beyond stalemate. Each party in the assembly had equal representation at the negotiation table, essentially levelling the playing field, which encouraged parties, such as Nidaa Tounes and the Popular Front, which had boycotted the assembly, to enter the process with confidence. Making government-handover negotiations conditional on the successful resolution of outstanding issues constitutional debate helped bring Ennahda and other members of its coalition to the table. As important as the framework was, the willingness of the two political leaders, Beji Caid Essebsi and Rached Ghannouchi, to sit together – first in private and then at the widely publicised National Dialogue signing ceremony – proved essential to concluding the process. These steps helped reassure the public that these two longtime rivals were committed to compromise and finding a way forward that would accommodate both camps. The constitution was finalised by an overwhelming majority in a celebrated televised vote in January 2014. The National Dialogue leadership and process have been heralded by Tunisian and international stakeholders as critical to ensuring the country's delicate transition – so much so that the quartet was awarded the 2015 Nobel Peace Prize.

The parliamentary and presidential elections proceeded from late October until December 2014. While Nidaa Tounes won the highest number of seats in parliament (86 of 217) and secured the presidency for Essebsi following a competitive run-off poll, the party's leaders again returned to the tradition of coalition negotiations to appoint a cabinet. Despite early indications to the contrary, Nidaa Tounes opted for a 'grand coalition' including its strongest rivals, Ennahda – which had come second in the parliamentary elections, with 69 seats, and had chosen early on not to run a presidential candidate – along with the Popular Front and Afek Tounes, which had been close allies during the turbulent 2013 period. This choice reflected both an acknowledgement of a closely contested series of elections and the challenges that lie ahead for Tunisia's political elite.

The way forward

Tunisia has survived the important first chapters of its transition, aided by its unique brand of pluralism and a balance of power between key political factions. With a constitution in place and an elected president and parliament, it now must face the chronic concerns that prompted the revolution in the first place, particularly the lack of jobs and economic opportunity, and the rise of extremism and security threats.

Human rights and judicial reform in the context of security threats

Transitional justice was one of four priorities for the coalition government that emerged from the 2011 elections. Accordingly, a cabinet-level position was established to address a wide range of violations. In December 2013, a far-reaching transitional-justice law finally passed the NCA, following two years of consultations that included victims and their families, along with members of civil society who had researched and advocated for human-rights protection. The law is meant to address violations committed since the establishment of the state, and includes the creation of the Truth and Dignity Commission to address national reconciliation and institutional reform, as well as reparations for victims and accountability through the judiciary.

While an important first step, the commission faces significant challenges ahead. It has been tasked with providing a special reparations fund for victims of alleged abuses and training a cadre of judges in the nuances of human-rights law. It also has an important role to play in encouraging, and overseeing, reforms within the security services. Cooperation within government institutions will be essential and by no means certain, given the corruption at all levels and the lack of a serious reform agenda since 2011.

Beyond rights-based reform, over the past four years Tunisia has struggled with a security sector oriented to protect state rather than citizens' interests, amid instability on its borders. Protecting the country's borders and addressing illegal trafficking of goods and arms, and growing radicalisation of segments of the population, while also building trust between citizens and armed services, will remain major challenges. In large measure, Tunisia's fate is of course linked to its immediate neighbours to the east and west. Democratically elected leaders will need to grapple with upholding constitutional values, including freedom of speech and association, while also protecting citizens against the threat from radicalised and armed groups within and beyond Tunisia's borders. These include the substantial number of Tunisians who have joined jihadists fighting in Iraq, Syria, and more recently in Libya.

This delicate balance was tested just months after elections, when in March 2015 terrorists attacked the Bardo Museum, a cultural landmark, and major tourist attraction, in the same grounds as the parliament, killing more than 20 people. The massacre was eerily repeated in June when a lone gunman murdered 38 people at beach resort in Sousse, most of them British tourists. To counter such threats in the future, Tunisia must both strengthen security institutions and undertake judicial reforms. This will enable the country to move away from Ben Ali's police state towards an evidence-based legal system. However, the political leadership's reaction to the Sousse attack appeared focused on reestablishing laws reminiscent of the old regime. The president declared a state of emergency and the parliament passed a harsh anti-terrorism law that human rights organisations criticised for giving too much authority to the security services at the expense of judicial oversight. How Tunisia balances the imperative to strengthen its security establishment with the values of respecting human rights that were at the core of the revolution will shape the future of its democracy.

Inclusive, democratic decision-making

Tunisia's political landscape is among the most diverse in the region, with two emerging power-brokers – Ennahda and Nidaa Tounes – surrounded by a smattering of smaller parties and prominent individuals contributing to the national debate. However, in almost all cases, these political elites – regardless of their affiliation – have focused on populist tactics, rather than finding policy solutions to the country's most pressing needs. In many respects, the period since January 2011 has been one of experimentation by political elites and parties. During the period leading up to NCA elections in 2011, party expectations about their electoral prowess were overwhelmingly ambitious and, in most cases, based on limited evidence. Election results confirmed the high degree of organisation and coordination within Ennahda's ranks, compared to the weaker performance of secular parties. Since then, some parties have developed internal organisation and member discipline. Others have adapted their communications with the public, focusing on more direct voter contact, in addition to national media. However, according to NDI public-opinion research, while parties may be diversifying their forms of communication, they continue to miss the mark and do not yet provide much policy content.

There are, therefore, opportunities not only to improve how parties engage voters, but also how they construct policies to respond to citizens' concerns. Adhering to democratic procedures (elections for party positions, quotas for under-represented populations, consultative bodies that inform decisions) and embracing direct contact with voters to listen and learn about their issues are two areas where Tunisian political parties can improve.

Moreover, parties can focus on improving the political participation of a youth population that is increasingly frustrated by what it views as little improvement in daily life since the revolution. Young Tunisian men and women find themselves left behind by the political process, with little motivation to join a political party, let alone choose one to vote for.

Local and regional elections, mandated by the constitution and slated to take place as early as autumn 2015, will be an important bellwether. Unlike presidential and parliamentary elections, these elections are viewed as the true milestone for democracy taking root, according to a majority of participants in the NDI research. Municipalities and locally elected officers are citizens' most direct contact with their government, and are responsible for addressing basic issues that influence quality of life.

Delivering on calls for reform

One of the greatest deceptions of Ben Ali's propaganda was that Tunisia was a beacon for prosperity and an economic model for North Africa. The country has the highest rate of youth unemployment in the region – a key driver of protests in 2008 and 2010 and ongoing frustration in the years since. Tunisia's newly elected president, parliament and government have a five-year mandate to not only tackle a sluggish market hampered by bureaucracy and generations of corruption, but also to consider reforms in education and healthcare, to meet public demand. The IMF's US$1.75 billion stand-by arrangement and other external assistance are intended to promote such reforms, stabilise Tunisia's fiscal position and encourage growth and job creation – critical issues for the country's democratic transition.[8]

Such assistance can only complement Tunisia-driven reforms. Candidates campaigned throughout the autumn of 2014, making a range of promises, from reducing trade barriers – with an overhaul of the import tax and customs systems – to revising banking and currency restrictions. However, it remains to be seen how Nidaa Tounes will follow up on these pledges, given that its benefactors during the campaign were business owners who had benefitted from Ben Ali-era practices. Also complicating necessary reforms is the traditional expectation of readily available public-sector jobs that the government can no longer afford. Instead, the government would be wise to ease bureaucratic requirements that hinder entrepreneurship and make capital more easily accessible for the private sector, where lending has traditionally been a recurrent source of corruption.

Just after the 2014 elections, Tunisians expressed their commitment to democratic values, but also voiced concern about their newly elected leaders' ability or interest to make difficult reforms. Addressing high unemployment and rising inflation in the immediate future were most often mentioned as key indicators that the new government was serious about translating campaign promises into tangible action.[9]

Tunisia's young democracy should not only be judged by the extent to which politicians drive a reform agenda, but also the degree to which the country's emboldened electorate pressures its leaders to do so, while respecting the hard-fought rights and liberties enshrined in the constitution, in the midst of security threats.

Notes

[1] Founded in 1946, UGTT has a membership of more than half a million and has played a prominent role in Tunisian politics since independence.

[2] Habib Boularès, *Histoire de La Tunisie: de la Préhistoire à la Révolution* (Tunis: Cérès Éditions, 2011).

[3] Michael Willis, *Politics and Power in the Maghreb: Algeria, Tunisia and Morocco from Independence to the Arab Spring* (New York: Hurst & Co., 2012).

[4] Peter J. Schraeder and Hamadi Redissi, 'Ben Ali's Fall,' *Journal of Democracy*, vol. 22, no. 3, July 2011, pp. 5–19.

[5] Nicole Rowsell and Asma Ben Yahia, 'Revolution to Reform: Citizen Expectations on the One-Year Anniversary of the Tunisian Uprising', National Democratic Institute, January 2012, https://www.ndi.org/files/NDI%20Tunisia-FG-Report-Jan2012-ENG.pdf.

[6] NDI public-opinion research noted that voters in 2011 who had chosen Ennahda cited the following reasons: a definitive break with the previous regime; a track record of struggle; and potential to address corruption going forward.

[7] Meaning 'compass' in English, Al Bawsala was created just after the assembly elections in 2011, with the goal of creating accountability of elected officials and increasing access to information on the part of Tunisian citizens.

[8] See Chapter Six.

[9] 'Following 2014 Elections, NDI Focus Group Research Shows Tunisians Optimistic About Democratic Transition', National Democratic Institute, 17 March 2015, https://www.ndi.org/files/En%20NDI%20Research%20Findings%20-%20Tunisia%20January%202015.pdf.

CHAPTER TWO

Libya: From Euphoria to Breakdown

Borzou Daragahi

At the very centre of the Libyan capital of Tripoli, adjacent to both the ancient Ottoman-era medina and the elegant Italian-built colonial district, lies Martyrs' Square. It was on this wide, paved plaza, then called Green Square, that Colonel Muammar Gadhafi's supporters gathered in defiant demonstrations, amid NATO air-strikes, during the 2011 bombing campaign. Six months later, tens of thousands of Libyans streamed in joyously to the same square to celebrate Gadhafi's downfall. But on one Friday in June 2014 the square became a battleground between those very Libyans who celebrated together in the summer and autumn of 2011. The outbreak of civil war can perhaps be traced to this particular moment, which illustrated how rival camps prioritised their desire for power over a collective commitment to building a new Libyan state.

The geography of the square that Friday morning reflected the political infighting and its potential dangers. On the north side of the square stood the Islamists, who in a startling emulation of their counterparts in Egypt, called themselves supporters of 'legitimacy'. On the south side were a few hundred men supporting the Gen. Khalifa Haftar's so-called 'Dignity' movement, which a month earlier had launched a war to destroy the Islamist militias in Benghazi.

At first the pro- and anti-Haftar crowd mostly threw water bottles and taunted each other. 'The blood of the martyrs will not be spilt in vain,' they shouted. 'Libya! Libya!' With both sides mostly chanting the same slogans, it might have been comical except for the armed men in camouflage on either side of the square, ostensibly providing security. On the west side of the square were men from the pro-Haftar Central Security branch of the Ministry of Interior. On the east side were men from one of the major pro-Islamist militias, Nawasi, from the eastern side of the capital. 'The balance of power may go back and forth', observed Abdullah Salem Shoma, a police officer watching the melee from the steps of the Ottoman fortress overlooking the square, 'but the stronger side will be the one who takes the square by force.'[1]

When the inevitable gunfire rang out, one man was shot in the leg; several people were wounded, one fatally. But the crowds did not clear. The fighting became more intense. Some of the Haftar supporters raised posters of the retired general alongside Egypt's strongman Abdel Fattah el-Sisi, whipping the Islamists into a frenzy. They attacked fiercely, pushing the Haftar supporters out of the square. But minutes later, the Haftar faction, bolstered by supporters from the nearby Fashloum district, stormed back into the square, driving out the Islamists in a dangerous show of street theatre that illustrated Libya's political and security crisis. Mohamed Salah Drah, a human-rights lawyer and civil-society activist later described the events on the square as a bleak milestone in the country's post-revolutionary history: 'What happened in the square that day was a disaster. What makes it even worse is that until this moment they don't know who fired the shots. If Libyans don't come to an accord, what happened in the square is going to happen to the country.'[2]

Libyans never came to such an accord, and the drama that unfolded in Martyrs' Square foreshadowed what would unfold in the rest of the country. The conflict that began in May 2014 with the Haftar supporters' attack on Islamist militias in Benghazi spread across Libya, leaving at least 4,000 people dead by October 2015 and entire neighbourhoods in ruins.[3] Tens of thousands of Libyans and long-time Egyptian and Tunisian residents fled their homes, joining millions of Syrians and Iraqis displaced by conflict. The chaos savaged Libya's once-promising economy, slashing oil production to a fraction of its post-revolution high of 1.4 million barrels per day and draining once overflowing public coffers to pay public salaries.[4] Amid the chaos, Abu Bakr al-Baghdadi's Islamic State of Iraq and al-Sham (ISIS) arrived. Aided by returnees from Syria and Iraq and boosted by the popularity of Wahhabi-inflected, puritanical Salafi ideology among some Libyan revolutionary fighters, ISIS, and groups pledging loyalty to it, began to launch terror attacks across Libya by late 2014. Its ranks numbered 3,000 and rising by March 2015.[5]

The chaos in Libya also fostered often deadly human trafficking. Already meagre efforts at interdicting truckloads of migrants crossing the country's borders faltered, leaving thousands to board rickety boats to make the perilous journey across the Mediterranean.[6]

The Libyan rebels who ousted Gadhafi with the help of NATO airstrikes knew that the road ahead would be hard; the transition from a bleak four-decade dictatorship to a politically open and pluralistic nation would be rough, slow and filled with bumps along the way. But unlike its neighbours Egypt and Tunisia, Libya potentially had hundreds of billions of dollars-worth of potential oil and gas reserves beneath its mostly desert terrain, as well as tens of billions tucked away in cash reserves and portfolio investments. It was not far-fetched to believe that the transition would be relatively smooth, and that new institutions could be built, forging a prosperous nation grounded in the rule of law. Even as late as July 2012, just after the country's first parliamentary elections, hope persisted. At his seaside compound in western Tripoli, Husni Bey Husni, one of Libya's richest men, predicted a bright future for the country: 'We will prove to be a beacon of democracy. We will surprise the world. We will be the model for all energy rich Arab countries. We have proven everybody to be wrong about us.'[7]

Back then, few imagined the horrors that would ultimately ensue. Armed gangs calling themselves revolutionaries held sway over the government and battled across the capital. A vicious assassination campaign by suspected extremist Islamist militias targeted police, soldiers, judges, clerics and activists. Hundreds died in ethnic and tribal clashes in the country's south. Amid the lawlessness and chaos, US Ambassador Christopher Stevens was murdered, and other foreign embassies and aid organisations were targeted.

In the years since the toppling of Gadhafi, Libya's nascent leadership has pursued an ever-growing feud at the expense of the country's faltering institutions. There seems to be no easy way out of the crisis, despite tenacious mediation efforts by United Nations' (UN) envoy Bernardino Leon and his predecessor, Tarek al-Mitri. The violence is partly fuelled by outside actors who – though publicly in support of a compromise – have frequently appeared more interested in defeating one side rather than throwing their weight behind a national dialogue or the UN's peace efforts.

The origins of chaos

The roots of Libya's current troubles stretch back to early in the uprising. Tensions seethed between military officials and technocrats who had defected from Gadhafi to join the revolution, and Islamists and outsiders who were fighting against a dictatorship that had barred them from participating in politics and civil society. The still-unsolved 29 July 2011 assassination, in the rebel-held east, of Abdul-Fattah Younes, a Gadhafi general who joined the uprising, should have set alarm bells ringing in Western capitals and among the National Transitional Council. The perpetrators of the crime were sought but what was ignored was the implication: the emergence of extremist Islamist militants seeking revenge for prior regime abuses and the elimination of any potential liberal or nationalist rivals.

'We have people who are trying to destroy the project of the new Libya and establishing their own state by using violence and trying to control the state', said Saleh Merghani, a long-time human-rights activist who served as justice minister in the post-revolutionary cabinets of premiers Ali Zidane and Abdullah Thinni. 'People lose their lives. We have bombings, deterioration of the security situation, and the draining of financial resources of the country to fight this war.'[8]

Within weeks of Tripoli's liberation, political jostling for power began, quickly displacing serious efforts to build state institutions from the top of the agenda. Mahmoud Jebril, a management consultant who had worked with the Gadhafi regime but later became the revolutionary government's interim prime minister, arrived in the capital and warned other political factions to stop their infighting, a move that only convinced his Islamist and Misratan rivals that he was seeking to entrench himself. Tribal alliances began to come to the fore as each faction sought to solidify its hold on the instruments of power and wealth, such as oil facilities, air- and seaports, government buildings, key roadways and smuggling routes.

The city of Zintan, although a staunch supporter of the revolution, has close kinship ties to the Wurfulla tribe (Libya's largest), counts Jebril as a member and served as a pillar of the Gadhafi regime. Misratans, residents of Libya's third-largest city, who bore some of the worst fighting in 2011, harbour longstanding animosity towards the Wurfulla. They formed an alliance with Islamist militias that sought to expunge former members of the Gadhafi regime from state institutions and public life.

Cultural differences also divided the relatively cosmopolitan urban intelligentsia, who may or may not have supported the revolution, and the mostly pious rural rebels who descended on the capital and other cities. Just weeks after Tripoli's liberation, medical staff at one hospital fumed at the militiamen regularly firing their weapons into the air in celebration or at each other in jousts over turf. One militia had taken over security at the facility, prompting a gunfight on the hospital grounds with a rival group.

Militia violence destroyed the country's political climate, despite the enthusiasm and energy of civil-society groups and news outlets that flowered after Gadhafi's overthrow. With each spurt of violence or anonymous threat posted on social media, non-governmental organisations (NGOs) and newspapers closed shop, relocating to Tunisia, Egypt or Europe, along with international organisations and diplomatic missions.

Across Libya, the surge in attacks on liberals and uniformed armed forces, along with the violence of Islamist militias, fuelled public enthusiasm for what later became Haftar's cause. This was particularly the case for those who saw the revolution as an opportunity to expand freedoms, rather than creating an Islamic utopia.

Revolution versus counter-revolution

The results of the 2012 elections for the General National Congress (GNC) shocked Libya's Islamists. They had bought into the myth of Libyans as conservative Muslims who would support Islamist candidates, just as Tunisians and Egyptians had. Moreover, the rules had been set up to dilute the power of any one bloc in parliament; 80 seats were reserved for the nascent political parties, while 120 were reserved for candidates running as individuals. Nevertheless, it was clear that Jebril's National Forces Alliance, a loose coalition of liberals and former regime supporters, had soundly defeated the Justice and Construction Party, Libya's Muslim Brotherhood and nascent Islamist factions – including the Qatari-backed Watan Party, led by former Libyan Islamic Fighting Group leader Abdelhakim Belhaj. For Islamists, the results also vindicated more extremist groups, such as Ansar al-Sharia, which had refused to participate in the elections.

But the Islamists and their allies rallied after the elections and managed to gain the upper hand in parliament, infuriating their liberal rivals. Through parliamentary manoeuvring, they wooed unaffiliated or independent members of the 200-seat assembly and demanded the passage of the political isolation law, which bars top-ranking Gadhafi-era officials from positions in public service. The now much-maligned law was voted on as militiamen surrounded parliament, and there was reportedly never a full reading of its final version in the GNC. It appeared particularly aimed at banning Jebril and his allies from a future in Libyan politics. According to Ousama Otman-Assed, chief executive officer (CEO) of the Libyan Centre for Strategic and Future Studies, 'This caused a deep split in Libyan society. It was unfair to a large number of Libyans. Gadhafi was here 42 years. It's normal that people would carry out their duties. But the political parties all rushed into the isolation law. There was a lack of courage and wisdom.'[9]

Moreover, the live-televised 2013 coup against the elected Islamist government of Muhammad Morsi in Egypt and subsequent months of chaos wrought havoc on Libyans' psyche.

They began to view themselves through the prism of their larger neighbour. But unlike Tunisia, where Islamists and liberals looked at the Egyptian experience and worked hard to avoid such an outcome, the main political camps in Libya took exactly the wrong lessons from Egypt's *coup d'état*. Liberals sought to emulate their Egyptian counterparts by rallying around a general rooted in the former regime, while Islamists concluded they were in a life-or-death struggle.[10] After all but declaring a coup in February 2014 that was widely mocked, Haftar rallied forces that included tribes and members of the Gaddafi-era army and police. He launched an offensive against the Shura Council of Benghazi Revolutionaries, a collection of Islamist militias that included Ansar al-Sharia, in May.[11] It was at this point that Libya's civil war began in earnest.

Until mid-2014, both factions controlled different pockets of the capital. But once Haftar's eastern offensive appeared to have inspired allies in the west, and particularly after the June elections had shown an overwhelming number of Libyans supported candidates opposed to the Islamists and allied regional militias,[12] the Islamists struck. Led by battle-hardened Misratan commanders, such as Salah Badi,[13] they launched a devastating attack on rival militias in the capital, pushing Zintan-rooted groups out, destroying the city's international airport, which was the Zintan militias' main stronghold, and seizing control of much of Tripoli, despite a series of air-strikes launched in support of Haftar allies by the UAE and possibly Egypt.

Solidifying the opposing camps

After three years of ever-shifting alliances, the outbreak of fighting over Tripoli in 2014 clearly delineated post-Gadhafi Libya into two broad camps: Dawn and Dignity. These camps hardened in the months after the elections, not only because of the blood spilt, but also over a fundamental disagreement about who has the legal right to rule.

The internationally recognised government in Tobruk insisted that it had won the elections fairly, and that those political forces opposing the Islamist and Misrata coalition had won three elections, including one in February for a constitutional assembly, led by Ali Tarhouni, a liberal. Nevertheless, the Islamists managed, through a combination of procedural wrangling, disbarring of candidates and outright intimidation by armed allies, to retain significant power. 'They set the rules of the game. We played by their rules and we beat them, but they never accepted it', said Hammouda Siala, a liberal and spokesman of the National Forces Alliance, the organisation once led by Jebril. 'They started to create a monopoly on power.'[14]

The political wing of the Dawn coalition consisted of members of the expired GNC, gathered in Tripoli, who insisted that they remained the legitimate political authority in Libya. They argued that the newly elected parliament had committed a 'coup against the 17 February revolution'[15] when 158 of 188 parliamentarians attended a swearing-in ceremony in Tobruk, ignoring demands by the outgoing Islamist-backed head of parliament to hold the proceedings in the capital, or Benghazi as originally intended by the transition roadmap. Their position was strengthened by a mysterious November 2014 constitutional court ruling that invalidated parts of the June election law (itself written by the expired GNC), but failed to spell out any legal consequences. Backed by their armed militias, the pro-Islamist and Misrata members of the GNC continue to govern from the capital, with full access to most institutions of the state, including the Central Bank and headquarters of the National Oil Corporation. The Tobruk and Baida-based eastern government was recognised by much of the world, but struggled to establish relevance on the ground.

The Dawn camp includes the powerful Misrata militias, the Libyan Muslim Brotherhood, and remnants of the former Libyan Islamic Fighting Group, a one-time al-Qaeda affiliate whose ageing members have reinvented themselves as politicians and leaders of 'revolutionary brigades', or militias. In addition to Amazighs (ethnic Berbers) who oppose Haftar's Arab nationalist pretensions, they are allied with the Islamist-led militias that dominate eastern Libya, and have tolerated extremists, such as Ansar al-Sharia and the Salafi-leaning Libyan Revolutionaries Operations Room. The camp, which influential Qatar-based cleric Ali Sallabi calls the 'Islamist national coalition'[16], retained strong influence over the GNC and many official bodies of government through a series of compromises made by successive premiers Abdurrahman Keib, Zidane and Thinni.

Haftar's sympathisers included all those who despise the Islamists, not so much for the values they espouse as for long-standing bad blood, suspicions of their ultimate intentions and fundamental disagreements over the Islamists' notion that revolutionary zeal must continue throughout the transition period. 'The time of revolution is over', said Hamed Mohamed, a member of the military council of Zintan, during a June 2014 interview. 'Now is the time to rebuild. We have to treat all Libyans equally.'[17]

In addition to elements of Gadhafi-era armed forces, they include powerful Zintan-rooted militias, namely Qhaqha, Madani and Suwaig, as well as eastern tribes that support a federal break-up of the country.

Both alliances are riddled with potentially destabilising contradictions. Misratans are no more conservative Muslims than Zintanis, and their alliances with the Islamists against Haftar and his ambitions may be less about ideology than interests. Misratans have bristled at some of the more extremist Islamists in their ranks, and even began taking on ISIS militants, while many liberals in Tobruk quickly grew uncomfortable with Haftar's imperious ways. Eastern federalists are even more suspicious of Haftar, and have spoken out against him; he, in turn, has deprived them of on-the-ground support in their battles against Misratan militias over oil facilities.

There is a regional dimension to the conflict. After initially staying on the sidelines, the UAE and Egypt came to strongly back Haftar and the elected government in Tobruk as part of their drive against what they perceive as the Muslim Brotherhood's regional ambitions. Early in the civil war they launched air-strikes to bolster the Dignity movement,[18] and later reportedly supplied munitions and refurbished aircraft.[19] Meanwhile the Islamist and Misrata-led camp looked to Turkey, Qatar and Sudan, which have been accused of shipping weapons to Libya Dawn.[20]

But there is little evidence that foreign weapons, influence or pressure have played a pivotal role in the struggle; the battle for Libya has largely been a Libyan affair. Each side has clung to its own narrative of righteousness. The supporters of Haftar and the House of Representatives in Tobruk accuse the Islamists of holding the nation captive, using their armed proxies to impose their agenda on the country, regardless of election outcomes or popular will. The Misratans and Islamists accuse their opponents of being dupes of the former regime, seeking to foment a counter-revolution, like that in Egypt, and profit from a revolution, for which their brigades have experienced the most intense fighting.

Although subtle, an ideological divide also separates the two camps. As one Western diplomat put it, 'It's about the role of Islam in politics, not about the role of Islam in private life. Everybody goes to the mosque, abides by sharia and accepts sharia. But one side says there is a role for Islam in politics and the others just don't want that.'[21]

Topography of fear

Libya's conflict has become more than ideological; it is also about the interest and relative power of different groups – and a fear of losing that power. The example of warlord Ibrahim Madani illustrates the fears of those in the Dignity camp. Madani, who is 30 years old, planned to leave the militia business in 2012, publicly handing over many of his men's weapons in a televised event meant to encourage other militias to do the same. The son of a famous Zintani fighter who was killed in battle when he rose up against Gadhafi in 2011, Madani spent months running a grocery store. But his militia coalesced again as tensions rose, and he was drawn back into armed conflict as a supporter of Haftar.[22]

The Islamists, on the other hand, fear a return to Gadhafi-era repression. The rise of Haftar, seen as the second coming of Gadhafi combined with Sisi, has particularly rattled them. Ali Sallabi's personal history illustrates the narrative espoused by the Dawn camp. For decades, he and his family were hounded by Gadhafi's security forces, and most of them were driven into exile for their association with the Islamists. Sallabi spent eight years in a dungeon in Tripoli's infamous Abu Slim prison, and more than a decade in exile in Saudi Arabia, Sudan and Qatar. In his view, despite election results, now it is the turn of Sheikh Sallabi and his ilk to lead the nation. 'Most of the municipal council elections are won by the Islamist stream', he said. 'Two-thirds of the constitutional assembly are for the Islamist stream.'[23]

Crucially, Libya's third city of Misrata, with its arsenal of tanks and heavy guns, has become the ultimate guarantor of Dawn's grip on the capital. It is also vital to the camp's efforts to take over oil installations in the south and centre of the country. The city suffered tremendously during the 2011 war, bombarded for months by Gadhafi's forces. The trauma of the conflict gave Misratans both a sense of victimisation and a vast armed force. This has granted the city outsized influence as an arbiter of power. Misrata's elders have refused to cede their weapons to a government – elected or not – that hopes to reintegrate former members of Gadhafi's army and is now dominated by a strongman reminiscent of the late dictator.

Dawn's supporters accuse the parliament in Tobruk of striking a devil's bargain with Haftar, which has forced them into an uncertain alliance with the jihadists. Haftar's transparent power grabs and undermining of civilian authority make even some supporters in Tobruk fearful of his motives. Haftar is a uniquely polarising and controversial figure, drawing attention from the international community as well. NGO Human Rights Watch has accused Haftar's air force of having used illegal cluster munitions in bombings over central Libya and killed at least seven civilians in joint air-strikes with Egypt on Derna, following ISIS's killing of Egyptian Coptic Christians migrant labourers.[24] Western diplomats and international interlocutors have been frustrated with Haftar's Manichaean portrayal of the fight against Islamists, conflation of moderate Islamists with jihadist terrorists, lack of political acumen and constant underperformance on the battlefield. Nevertheless, the UN panel mandated to examine Libya's conflict 'could not confirm' that Haftar's actions had 'a decisive national spoiler effect and found little evidence to suggest that [his air force's] aerial bombardments had resulted in large numbers of civilian casualties'.[25]

A distinction must be made between the Islamist militias, including their allies in Misrata, and those in groups such as the Libyan Revolutionaries Operations Room in Tripoli or Ansar al-Sharia in the east. The problem is not the official militias per se, but the fact that they prevent the uniformed armed forces from doing their job holding back the extremists, especially in the east. 'Even if the authorised militias are not participating in bombings, they still want to prevent police and security from operating', said former justice minister, Saleh Merghani. 'They are providing a safe haven for terrorist groups.'[26]

Prospects for reconciliation

Victims of Libya's conflict include many who were on the front lines of the revolution and have sought to compromise peacefully in its aftermath. The June 2014 assassination of a well-regarded activist and lawyer, Salwa Bugaighis, by presumed jihadist militants and the February 2015 public execution of women's-rights activist Intisar al-Hasiri in a street in Tripoli, have shown how brutal the war has become. No one has answered for either murder nor have they been properly investigated.

Unfortunately, formal efforts to bring the two sides together have dragged on while the violence persists. Attempts by the UN Support Mission in Libya to host a dialogue on key national issues have yielded multiple drafts of a document setting out terms for establishing a Government of National Accord but little consensus. The UN special representative Benerdino Leon proposed an interim government that would include a presidency council consisting of a prime minister, three deputies and two additional representative government ministers, and a legislature made up of the previously elected House of Representatives and a Council of State that would serve as consultative body with a less clearly defined role. In October Leon proposed names to occupy the key positions of the unity government, but it remained unclear whether the parties would ratify his proposal.[27] Even if Leon succeeds in forging an agreement, the governing formula is based on consensus, which Libyans have not witnessed since the 2011 revolution.

With ISIS's rise and the country mired in civil war, the international community now frets about Libya, questioning NATO's involvement in the 2011 uprising, and whether the country would have been better off had Gadhafi been allowed to crush Benghazi as he was poised to do in March, when he was stopped and turned back by Western airpower. Some describe the increasingly complex political and security morass as inevitable once Gadhafi was toppled. But grave mistakes marred the post-transition period.

Arguably, the country would have been better off if the international community and Libyans had agreed to deploy UN peacekeepers or foreign troops on the ground – a credible force that could have taken control of weapons depots and maintained security until Libya's regular armed forces were strengthened.

The timeline for Libya's elections, set by the UN and agreed to by the National Transitional Council, moved too quickly,[28] before political parties had a chance to form and Libyans could develop political identities. Constitutional scholars, including Zaid al-Ali, who advised the Libyan authorities, say the country should have continued in a quasi-transitional mode until a constitution was written. 'The transitional plan was the most inept of all the countries', he said. 'Libya was the country that had the least in terms of state institutions. Yet a decision was made to rely very heavily on election results.'[29]

But most of the mistakes were made by Libyans themselves and can only be fixed by the country's own political leaders. Libya's weak governments have continued to cave in to the demands of militias. The very militias that have undermined the government's credibility, such as Nawasi and Madani in the west, or the February 17 and Rafallah al-Sahati brigades in the east, remain on government payrolls. And while each militiaman gets paid around US$1,000 a month, none of the interim governments have launched an employment or public-works programme to lure young men off the streets. Tens of billions of dollars a year are spent on wasteful food and fuel subsidies and a public sector that does little but push paper – rather than invested in the country's infrastructure or youth by bolstering education or healthcare. Despite Libya's vast financial resources, none of the interim governments post-Gadhafi have presented a credible weapons-buyback programme or made concrete efforts to bring weapons under national control.

Successive governments have dismissed demands by Libya's Amazigh, Touareg and Tebu ethnic minorities for basic language, cultural and citizenship rights, throwing away potentially valuable stakeholders in the country's democratic experiment. Despite promises, the bloated, ineffective public sector has not been reformed nor made more transparent, fuelling perceptions of continued corruption.

Politicians quickly formed alliances with like-minded militias, establishing a pattern since Gadhafi's overthrow of using their self-declared authority to give the gunmen official authorisation to bear arms. In return, militias protected the politicians from any harm, as when Misratans and Islamists prevented the Zintan brigades from taking over the capital's parliament in May 2014. Instead of building institutions, politicians have empowered gunmen to protect them.[30]

Tolerance of, and even support for, extremist militias by Islamists and some Misratans has provided the space for ISIS's rise in Libya. Not only do some groups, such as Ansar al-Sharia and the Salafi-jihadist Libyan Revolutionaries Operations Room[31], overlap ideologically with ISIS, but other less extreme militias prevent uniformed armed forces from doing their job, especially in the east; 'they are providing a safe haven for terrorist groups' according to Merghani[32].

Even pro-Dawn militias not affiliated with ISIS have pursued agendas frightening to liberals, driving them into Haftar's ranks. From its base in the Tripoli neighbourhood of Souk Joumeh, the Nawasi controls the coastal road east toward the strategic Mitiga air base, and arrests young people for suspected drug use or homosexuality. The Operations Room has long controlled the main coastal highway leading to Tunisia, where it terrorises passers-by for moral and political, as well as legal, offences. These militias see themselves as inheritors and defenders of the revolution and are focused on gaining control over formal institutions of power.

Influenced by events in neighbouring Egypt, Libya's political elite have become engaged in a nasty, reckless battle pitting the country's Muslim Brotherhood and its allies against their opponents. With their armies and long-standing institutions, Egypt and Tunisia have been able to withstand such infighting. But in fragile Libya it has meant the political class has set aside critical, time-sensitive issues around institution-building in a quest for power. According to one political commentator, 'The entire mindset was wrong. Because of this fight for power they traded in everything – from minority rights to disarming militias. A kind of vigilante atmosphere took hold. Scores were settled to get power.'[33]

The aims and fears of men with guns have darkened the country's future. Pressed to identify the primary culprit for Libya's deep troubles, Lt.-Col. Ahmed Ali, a commander of a pro-Dawn armed unit in Tripoli, demurred. 'To be honest they are all revolutionaries...We Libyans are one family, one tribe. But because of this fight for power we are losing everything.'[34]

Notes

1 Interview with police officer Abdullah Salem Shoma, Tripoli, June 2014.

2 For a video clip of the incident, see 'Martyrs Square, Tripoli, Libya, 6 June 2014', http://bit.ly/MartyrSquare.

3 Data compiled by Libya Body Count based on news reports; see www.libyabodycount.org.

4 Heba Saleh, 'Libya burns through foreign reserves to plug payments deficit', Financial Times, 11 December 2014.

5 Mark Hosenball, 'U.S. fears Islamic State is making serious inroads in Libya',Reuters, 20 March 2015.

6 Borzou Daragahi, 'Libya's chaos allows migrant numbers to surge', Financial Times, 20 April 2015.

7 Interview with Husni Bey Husni, Tripoli, July 2012.

8 Interview with Saleh Merghani, Tripoli, June 2014.

9 Interview with Ousama Otman-Assed, Tripoli, June 2014.

10 Egypt's Muslim Brotherhood has, in fact, few if any links to extremist, violent groups while ties between Libya's Brotherhood and jihadist groups are easily discernible.

11 Borzou Daragahi, 'Aircraft and artillery attack Islamist militias in Benghazi', Financial Times, 16 May 2014.

12 Mohamed Eljarh, 'Libya's Islamists Go for Broke', Foreign Policy, 22 July 2014; Caroline Abadeer, 'Libya's Election Results Announced', Muftah.org, 27 July 2014.

13 Borzou Daragahi, 'Hero of Libya's revolution wages war on government', Financial Times, 25 August 2014.

14 Interview with Hammouda Siala, Tripoli, June 2014.

15 Libya Al Ahrar TV, 4 August 2014.

16 Interview with Ali Sallabi, Tripoli, Libya, June 2014.

17 Interview with Hamed Mohamed, Libya, June 2014.

18 David D. Kirkpatrick and Eric Schmitt, 'Arab Nations Strike in Libya, Surprising U.S.', New York Times, 25 August 2014, http://www.nytimes.com/2014/08/26/world/africa/egypt-and-united-arab-emirates-said-to-have-secretly-carried-out-libya-airstrikes.html?_r=0.

19 See 'Final report of the Panel of Experts submitted pursuant to resolution 1973 (2011)', submitted to the UN Security Council, 23 February 2015, pp. 36–43.

20 Chris Stephen, 'Libya Accuses Khartoum of Flying Weapons to Islamist Rebels in Tripoli', Guardian, 7 September 2014, http://www.theguardian.com/world/2014/sep/07/libya-khartoum-weapons-islamist-rebels; 'Libyan PM says Qatar sent arms to opposition', Al Jazeera, 15 September 2014, http://www.aljazeera.com/news/middleeast/2014/09/libyan-pm-says-qatar-sent-arms-opposition-20149158050556226.html. See also, 'Final report of the Panel of Experts submitted pursuant to resolution 1973 (2011)', submitted to the UN Security Council, 23 February 2015, pp. 43–5.

21 Interview with Western diplomat in Tripoli, June 2014.

22 Interview with Ibrahim Madani, Tripoli, June 2014.

23 Interview with Ali Sallabi, Tripoli, June 2014.

24 Human Rights Watch, 'Libya: Evidence of New Cluster Bomb Use', 15 March 2015; Human Rights Watch, 'Libya/Egypt: Civilian Toll in Derna Air Strikes', 24 February 2015.

25 'Final report of the Panel of Experts submitted pursuant to resolution 1973 (2011)', submitted to the UN Security Council, 23 February 2015, p. 15.

26 Interview with Saleh Merghani, Tripoli, June 2014.

27 Names of Government of National Accord Proposed: Excerpts from SRSG Bernardino Leon's Press Conference in Skhirat, Morocco, 8 October 2015 http://unsmil.unmissions.org/Default.aspx?tabid=3543&ctl=Details&mid=6187&ItemID=2099277&language=en-US

28 Randa Takieddine, 'Former UN envoy: Libya held its elections too soon', Al Monitor, 12 October 2014.

29 Podcast interview with Zaid al-Ali, 'FT News special: What went wrong with the Arab Spring?', 26 January 2015.

30 Ahmed Elumami and Ulf Laessing, 'Gunmen loyal to ex-general storm Libyan parliament, demand suspension', Reuters, 18 May 2014.

31 Borzou Daragahi, 'Government-aligned militia adds to Libya's political turmoil', *Financial Times*, 25 July 2014.

32 Interview with Saleh Merghani, Tripoli, June 2014.

33 Bourzou Daragahi, 'Libya pays the price for its post-Gaddafi mistakes', *Financial Times*, 17 March 2014.

34 Interview with Lt.-Col. Ahmed Ali, Joint Cooperation Force, Tripoli, June 2014.

CHAPTER THREE

Power and Authority in Morocco

Haim Malka

In December 1990 tens of thousands of Moroccans filled the streets of Fes and smaller cities across the country.[1] Organised protests quickly turned to riots. The rioters were mostly young, many of them unemployed university graduates, frustrated by socio-economic hardship, lack of opportunity and poor job prospects.[2] King Hassan II responded forcefully at first. In the ensuing violence, security forces killed more than 30 people and arrested more than 200 in Fes alone.[3] But Hassan II's response evolved. In the following years, he acknowledged mounting public calls for greater political, civil and economic rights and launched a series of managed political and constitutional reforms.[4] The Fes riots were not the first time that Moroccans had taken to the streets in protest. But it was the first time that protests led to such direct constitutional changes.

Almost exactly two decades after those riots, in February 2011, tens of thousands of Moroccans took to the streets again in 53 cities across the country. The protesters called to amend the constitution, limit the king's powers and end corruption. They also called for justice and dignity. Their message was clear: they wanted change. Most of the protesters had come of

age at a time when mass media and information were changing the way people throughout the region thought about their
rights as citizens. After seeing the power of popular demonstrations to change regimes in Egypt and Tunisia only weeks
earlier, many Moroccans were hopeful and fearless. Except for
several isolated incidents, security forces allowed protesters
to march peacefully with little interference.[5] King Mohammed
VI, who had ruled for over a decade since the death of his
father Hassan II in 1999, responded quickly. Seventeen days
after the first protests, he addressed the nation on television,
promising 'comprehensive constitutional reform' and a 'new
charter between the throne and the people'.[6] The most significant constitutional reforms included a mandate that the prime
minister would be chosen from the largest political party, and
Morocco's indigenous Amazigh language would be established as an official language alongside Arabic.

The king's response stabilised a volatile situation at a time
when regimes in Tunisia, Egypt and Libya were crumbling. His
actions followed a pattern by Morocco's monarchy of adapting
to public pressure in order to maintain stability and survive.
While the monarchy uses coercive mechanisms and co-opts
elites, similar to other regimes, its most powerful tool in the
past two decades has been managing a process of gradual political reform. The reforms have attempted to satisfy just enough
public discontent while maintaining a monopoly of executive
power in religious, political, diplomatic and security affairs.

Although Mohammed VI's response to popular uprisings
in 2011 has mostly succeeded, it has revived a persistent question of whether gradual, palace-driven reforms from above can
produce tangible institutional change in how power is shared
and exercised. For Moroccans eager to see their country change,
the process appears to be endless. What will Moroccans call for
in one, five or ten years from now?

The challenge is that the reforms carried out may – if they are successful – only partially address the frustrations under-pinning protests since the 1990s. While the king's response to popular uprisings has focused on constitutional and parlia-mentary reforms, core public grievances, especially among young people, centre on an unequal system characterised by corruption, favouritism and lack of opportunity. What many young Moroccans want – dignity and justice – are intangible and difficult to measure, let alone deliver. But without address-ing these popular demands, the future will remain turbulent.

The nature of authority and power

Once a year, for the past several centuries, Morocco's notable family heads, senior civil servants and tribal representatives gather in one of the king's palaces. Assembled in neat rows and wearing traditional clothes, they wait for the monarch to emerge. Once he appears, each row of men bows and shouts an oath of allegiance (ba'ya) to the king. The annual ceremony reinforces the king's authority as the foundation of the Moroccan state and nation. That authority is based on both secular political rule, and his religious authority, as a descendant of the Prophet and his title of commander of the faithful (amir al-mu'minin).

For centuries, however, Morocco's kings or sultans faced opposition and have struggled to enforce that authority. Before independence in 1956, the struggle depended on the sultan's ability to collect taxes and raise armies from quasi-independent tribes in the hinterland.[7] Many tribes resisted, but even those that refused to pay and rejected the sultan's political authority still maintained contact with the sultan and acknowledged his religious lineage as a descendant of the Prophet.[8] Even if they resented his powers and violently resisted him at times, they did not question the monarchy as an institution. The debate, instead, was over the monarchy's appropriate political powers.

Today, the debate concerns the king's executive authority, the division of power between the monarchy and elected representatives in government and parliament, and the king's relationship with the Moroccan people.[9]

The monarchy's support base

The king can mobilise a range of support bases to promote his agenda, most importantly loyal political parties, business elites, civil-society groups, security services and religious institutions. For example, on the Friday prior to the 2011 constitutional referendum, the Ministry of Islamic Affairs reportedly issued instructions for imams to urge their congregants to vote, on religious grounds, in favour of the referendum. The king indirectly influences the editorial content of broadcast media by appointing the heads of all public radio and television stations. He can also direct economic resources to large-scale public initiatives, such as the National Initiative for Human Development (INDH) aimed at reducing poverty and the National Human Rights Council, created to support his reform agenda.

The security services and police are also an important tool, as they are in any system. During Hassan II's reign, known as the 'years of lead', the king used widespread force to intimidate and repress political opposition. Mohammed VI took a different approach when he ascended the throne, dismissing security chiefs and launching a process to publicise past abuses. However, following the 2003 Casablanca bombings, which killed 33 people, the security forces arrested between 2,000 and 5,000 people. Despite some improvements to the criminal justice system, allegations of torture in prisons and unfair or politically motivated trials persist. Regime opponents who cross unspoken red lines often find themselves in court on trumped-up charges that lead to jail or hefty fines. Unlike in many countries, however, in Morocco local and international organisations routinely document and publicise these complaints.

One of the monarchy's most important support bases is the circle of the ruling elite, referred to as the *makhzen*. It extends throughout the country from the palace's inner circle of advisers to regional governors and local officials appointed by the king. Through the *makhzen* the king and his royal advisers set political agendas and influence debates through pro-palace party elites, parliamentary committees, state-controlled media, security services and business allies.

Managed reform

The king's response to demands for change in 2011 was swift, making full use of his sources of influence. In the days after his 9 March speech he called for new elections, released nearly 200 prisoners arrested after the 2003 Casablanca bombings, and appointed a committee to draft a series of constitutional amendments.[10] It was the most sweeping set of political changes of his rule.

A hastily arranged constitutional referendum was passed in July 2012, followed by parliamentary elections in November.[11] The king appointed Abdelilah Benkirane, head of Morocco's Islamist Justice and Development Party (PJD), to form the new government, after his party won the largest share of votes.[12] It was not the first time the king had appointed an opposition party to lead,[13] but it was the first Islamist one in Morocco's history. What also made this case different was that, under the new constitution, Mohammed VI was now obligated to allow the PJD to form the new government; he could no longer use an ill-defined executive authority to name someone.

Morocco's 2011 constitution built on Mohammed VI's earlier reforms that centred on improving women's rights and investigated past regime abuses. These efforts further supported the monarchy's democratisation and human rights agenda.[14] During this period, public debate and political space expanded on a range of sensitive subjects in unprecedented ways. A 2008 initiative on regionalisation also sought to empower local and regional governments, which remains an ongoing effort.

The country's reform process has combined progress on human rights and representative governance with traditional ways of exerting authority, including occasionally coercion, silencing dissent and using elite groups to promote the monarchy's decisions and agenda.[15] This strategy has been in part to enlist as many constituencies as possible to participate in the process. Unlike regimes in other parts of the region, which provide little or no space for political activism, Morocco's monarchy recognises the importance of sharing political space within boundaries, including with Islamist movements. By giving different segments of the population a stake in the process, the monarchy has been able to build a broad consensus for its gradual reforms and legitimise its actions.

Despite its limits, Morocco's reform process has generated robust public debate about the separation of powers. From this perspective, Morocco's reform process does not have a finish line by design. The monarchy reacts and adjusts to pressure when necessary in order to maintain equilibrium and preserve its powers.

Pressure points

Since independence in 1956, the monarchy's authority has steadily grown. Nevertheless, it is not immune to political pressure from opposition parties, powerful families, trade unions, civil society, independent media and grassroots activists. It constantly assesses public sentiment in order to accommodate these constituencies in different ways. The king has been able to manage these different groups and maintain stability in part because they have different demands and objectives, which the monarchy can respond to with different tools and policies.

Political opposition has traditionally emerged from three broad sources: political parties, which work through parliamentary politics; non-parliamentary Islamists; and civil-society or grassroots organisations. Morocco boasts over 30 political parties, most of which support the status quo. Some parties, such as the PJD, seek to slowly rebalance power from the monarchy to elected representatives. Very few want to radically alter the political and economic status quo by limiting the king's executive powers. Morocco also has a diverse and active civil society that advocates issue-specific policies, which often push the limits of public debate on nearly every issue facing the country. At times, these broad constituencies for reform overlap and share similar objectives.

Opposition within limits

By the 1990s most of Morocco's parties largely accepted the king's dominant role in Moroccan politics and decision-making. They either worked to promote the palace's agenda or posed no serious challenge to monarchical rule. The king successfully co-opted the Istiqlal Party, which led Morocco's independence movement, and later the Socialist Union of Popular Forces (USFP), which headed the government from 1997–2002. Both political threats were neutralised by giving them a stake in the parliamentary system, along with the prestige of heading the government, even with constrained powers. Only a handful of small leftist parties continue to call for a parliamentary monarchy in which the king's powers would be tightly constrained.

The PJD has been the greatest source of parliamentary opposition in the past decade. Whereas most political parties are ideologically indistinguishable from one another, the PJD is well organised, disciplined, has a clear conservative ideological agenda and, most importantly, has a vision for Morocco, which it calls the 'third way'. Rather than advocating revolutionary change or the status quo, the PJD sees slow, deliberate reform as the most effective strategy to shift the balance of power in favour of parliament and elected government, and away from the palace. This strategy involves three main phases. Firstly, political parties focus on modest social and economic changes. Next, the government and parliament work toward strengthening national institutions and improving accountability and transparency. In the final phase, the balance of power between the monarchy and elected government will shift in the government's favour.[16] While the PJD sees a role for the monarchy in Morocco's future, it is a monarchy vested with a more symbolic role rather than wielding executive authority in policymaking.

For the moment the palace has neutralised the PJD as an immediate threat. It allowed the PJD to form a political party and compete in the 1997 parliamentary elections at a time when Islamists in neighbouring countries were denied entry into formal politics.[17] Unlike other Moroccan Islamists, most importantly the al-Adl wal-Ihsan (Justice and Charity) movement, the PJD accepts the king's religious role as commander of the faithful and the importance of the monarchy as a unifying national institution. Integrating the PJD in the 1990s not only broadened the political space and competition, but also prevented religion from becoming a source of political opposition and conflict as it was in neighbouring countries. Moreover, it more clearly divided Islamists between those who accept monarchical rule and those who reject it. This distinction is the dividing line between political participation and exclusion.

The PJD election victory in 2011 cemented the palace's co-optation of the movement by allowing the party to head the government and carry the burden that came with it. The PJD went from an opposition party that challenged the government to condemning the February 20 demonstrators and defending the king in numerous venues. In doing so, the party hoped to demonstrate its support for the monarchy and silence any uncertainty about its loyalty. Given that the king sets the pace of reform, the party's strategy now depends on cooperation with the palace.

By heading a government with monarchical oversight, the PJD has become a convenient scapegoat for unpopular yet necessary economic policies such as subsidy and pension reform, which it has carefully started to implement as part of its commitments to the IMF. The PJD campaigned on promises of ending corruption, improving government transparency and services, and boosting economic growth and job creation. It has struggled at times, however, in part because it does not have the authority to shape government policies, which are set by the royal court. Early efforts to legislate media reforms, such as limiting alcohol advertisements and including the call to prayer on public broadcasting, sparked a backlash from pro-palace parties and the elite. Plans to investigate corruption have also been stonewalled. Despite these setbacks, the PJD overcame a coalition crisis in 2013 and remains popular as an authentic party that resonates with many people. It performed well in the September 2015 municipal and regional elections, especially in urban areas, where it demonstrated solid middle-class support. Its future role and success, however, will depend not only on whether it can meet the expectations of its voters and demonstrate progress on its core issues, but also on its ongoing accommodation with the palace.

Non-parliamentary Islamists

Al-Adl wal-Ihsan, a popular grassroots Islamic movement that rejects the king's political and religious authority (and therefore does not participate in parliamentary politics), remains a long-term challenge to the monarchy. Because it does not compete in elections, it is difficult to gauge the movement's size and popularity, but it is widely believed to be one of the largest social-political movements in the country. Al-adl wal-Ihsan rejects violence as a strategy, but has a revolutionary vision for a new political and social order in Morocco without the monarchy. After the death in 2012 of its charismatic leader, Abdessalam Yassine, the movement debated whether to enter formal politics. For the moment, it has rejected the Moroccan political system and is not likely to pose a direct challenge. Instead, al-Adl wal-Ihsan will probably continue building grassroots support for its anti-monarchy message.

Salafists are also active and increasingly visible in Morocco.[18] After cracking down on them following deadly bombings in Casablanca in 2003, the king began pardoning leading Salafist sheikhs in 2011–12. This strategy allows greater space for Salafists, as long as they demonstrate loyalty to the monarchy, and it further divides the Islamist opposition. One sheikh, Mohammed Fizazi, for example, who had been sentenced to 30 years in prison for his links to the Casablanca bombings, declared his support for the monarchy after his release.[19] Whether Salafist preachers remain apolitical or not, non-violent Salafists are likely to remain part of Morocco's future religious and social landscape.

New coalitions

The 2011 uprisings created new and diverse coalitions demanding fundamental and immediate change. In 2011, for example, the February 20 movement emerged when young activists, inspired by events in Tunisia and Egypt, called for a day of action and protest. Unlike previous efforts to rally young activists through social media, on that Sunday in February tens of thousands gathered in cities across Morocco. Many of the organisers came from middle-class backgrounds, and some had experience working for civil-society organisations. Crucially, the February 20 movement tapped into a growing phenomenon of online activism by previously disengaged young people, which focused on specific causes, such as police brutality and economic inequality.

February 20's initial strength came from its success in uniting both secular and Islamist activists. The youth wing of al-Adl wal-Ihsan joined the movement in its first year. Overall, more than 40 civil-society groups, including several political parties, joined the broad coalition. This included some of Morocco's established non-governmental organisations, such as the Moroccan Association of Human Rights (AMDH), al-Adl wal-Ihsan and extreme leftist political parties, including the Unified Socialist Party (PSU) and Anahj Democrati (Democratic Way). While a core group of young activists had launched the movement, it remained largely decentralised, with no clear national leadership structure.

The February 20 protesters initially laid out seven broad demands, which fell into two categories.[20] The first focused on power and authority. These demands called for: an elected constitutional committee that would draft a new constitution to enshrine popular sovereignty and place limits on the king's authority; the dismissal of parliament and the government; the creation of an independent judiciary; and the release of political prisoners. The second category called for socio-economic justice, equality and an end to corruption. February 20 also demanded that Amazigh be recognised as an official language along with Arabic. Ultimately, what Moroccans called for during those early protests of 2011 was a system in which the monarchy's political and economic power would be substantially diminished to a more symbolic role enshrined in law.

The limits of reform

Morocco's reforms have helped advance the debate on a range of issues and genuinely increased citizen participation, but they have not fundamentally altered the balance or separation of powers. More importantly, constitutional reforms only address part of Morocco's problems: namely, demands for greater political representation and participation. The reforms fail to address the favouritism, corruption and lack of opportunity that have created a marginalised and unemployed youth population with little chance of advancement. Without addressing these critical issues, popular protests will continue to threaten Morocco's stability.

Part of the challenge is that these problems are deeply ingrained in Morocco's social, economic and political structure. Although nearly all of the country's macroeconomic and human development indicators have improved over the last several decades, the numbers skew endemic and worsening problems, such as a growing income gap between rural and urban areas, poor public education and youth unemployment close to 30%. Access to healthcare remains unequal, especially between rural and urban areas, and between wealthy and poor populations.[21] Morocco is diversifying its economy away from overdependence on the agricultural sector, but greater economic growth has not translated into more jobs, and higher education does not necessarily help.

The king acknowledged these deep challenges in a speech marking Morocco's Throne Day in August 2013. In the speech, the king asked, 'Why is it that so many of our young people cannot fulfil their legitimate professional, material, and social aspirations?'[22] The speech bluntly acknowledged Morocco's deficiencies, especially its poor education system, but did not present a strategy to address them.[23] The following year the king marked the 15th anniversary of his rule with another speech that addressed social injustice and the income gap. He cited World Bank studies that indicated growing income and wealth in Morocco and asked: 'Where is this wealth? Has it benefited all Moroccans or only some segments of society?'[24] Speeches addressing these sensitive questions display confidence but also require a delicate balance. They seek to acknowledge and champion widespread problems, while also distancing the monarchy from culpability. However, they could also draw greater scrutiny of the monarchy's role in overseeing a system that perpetuates these challenges if such questions remain unanswered.

Unlike its neighbour Algeria or the Gulf Arab monarchies, Morocco does not have the financial resources to buy political stability by providing public-sector jobs or large-scale spending projects. Following the protests in 2011, the government raised civil-servant wages and almost tripled the stabilisation fund, which keeps the prices of consumer staple goods down. But subsidies, especially for fuel and basic commodities, carry a significant financial burden on state revenues, and Morocco has searched for practical ways to direct subsidies more effectively to the population that is most in need.

Moreover, given that the monarchy's power depends in part on its large elite patronage network, any attempt to redistribute wealth would meet fierce opposition from the monarchy's key support base. Morocco's elite system is similar to other societies where wealthy families dominate economic activity and pass wealth and privilege to their children. What is different in Morocco's case is the vestige of a feudal class system, which often impedes social mobility. Hard work and education are not enough to secure a job, let alone greater prosperity and financial security. Without connections and favours from powerbrokers, it is difficult to gain entry into prestigious schools, secure credit and business loans or enter the civil service.

Serious reforms would also have to systematically address Morocco's corruption, which limits the country's economic potential. In 2013, Transparency International ranked Morocco 97th out of 177 countries on its global corruption perception index and gave it a score of 37 out of 100.[25] Morocco suffers from two types of corruption: low-level transactional corruption, to secure administrative favours for basic services, including medical treatment, and larger-scale corruption based on securing public procurement contracts.

There are limits to how much power the monarchy is willing to devolve in order to preserve and protect its status. It is unclear how much more authority the monarchy will devolve to parliament in the future. What is clear is that the king's role as commander of the faithful is a non-negotiable foundation of the monarchy. Mohammed VI has redoubled efforts to define and shape Moroccan religious identity, by implementing a number of reforms in the religious sphere, intended to strengthen his religious leadership, and promote Islamic values that are tolerant and respect authority.[26] His March 2011 speech and the revised constitution make it clear that his religious role is 'sacred' and an 'immutable value', and his public speeches since then have continued to stress the importance of this.

The next wave?

The king's constitutional reform strategy in 2011 successfully outmanoeuvred and split the organised opposition, which had previously cooperated despite different agendas and objectives. Some of the protesters were satisfied with the modest reforms, while leftist activists continued calling for a parliamentary monarchy where the king's powers would be largely symbolic. Others, led by al-Adl wal-Ihsan, rejected the idea of the monarchy altogether and opposed any accommodation. By the close of 2011 al-Adl wal-Ihsan had ceased its cooperation with February 20, breaking the coalition between Islamists and secularists and ending the unified opposition – one of the biggest threats to the monarchy. Violence and uncertainty were growing in Tunisia, Libya, Egypt and Syria, and many Moroccans preferred the stability of the status quo to uncertainty. Protests continued, but were smaller in numbers, and the police increasingly used force against demonstrators. In 2014, a few hundred people gathered to commemorate the third anniversary of the February 20 movement, rather than the tens of thousands who had assembled before.

But dissent in Morocco continues; protests over a range of local issues are routine across the country. The immediate threat has been neutralised but not eliminated. Crucially, Morocco's grassroots opposition is more willing to openly criticise the king in new ways.

The post-February 20 opposition is being driven largely by outspoken journalists, artists, and activists who are committed to continuing a public debate over the king's powers. Many of the taboos have been broken, and many of these activists are pushing the limits. A young rap musician and activist known as al-Haqed (the enraged or indignant) was the public face of individual protest in 2013–14. His lyrics take aim at the security forces and monarchy, accusing them of corruption and supporting injustice.[27] The authorities have used the justice system to harass and punish journalists and artists who are critical of the monarchy. However, rather than silencing dissent, the authorities are attracting more attention to these activists and their message.

Other issue-specific protests and calls to action continue. In early August 2013, thousands of Moroccans protested after the king pardoned a Spanish citizen in jail for committing heinous crimes against children.[28] The royal cabinet issued a statement following the protests that the pardon was a mistake. A few days later, the king announced that he had reversed it. This was the first time the king had responded to a direct call to reverse an unpopular decision.

It would be shortsighted to view this as an isolated case. People have seen that public pressure, protest and specific calls for action can force the monarchy to make changes. Highly publicised incidents that highlight abuses of power or disregard for average citizens could potentially unite a broad cross-section of society, sparking off public protests and criticism. Such incidents would not only be difficult to contain, but would also make it increasingly difficult for the elected government to defend the king's actions, creating additional tension between government and monarchy.

The February 20 movement laid the foundation for a diverse network of organisers, activists and bloggers to build coalitions demanding change. While they have failed to connect their cause to broad-based national action, they have succeeded in keeping alive the debate on executive power.

Moreover, protests over socio-economic issues have become the norm in Morocco since 2011. One estimate in 2014 suggested that Morocco witnesses approximately 50 unrelated demonstrations every day throughout the country.[29] The largest protests, sometimes with up to several thousand people, are usually made up of unemployed youth and graduates.

So far, opposition groups disagree over ideology, priorities and objectives. Divisions between secularists and Islamists that were bridged in early 2011 have deepened again. Protesters' demands vary; most want jobs and better access to services such as education, healthcare and housing. Some demand a parliamentary monarchy where the king has more ceremonial authority. Others, chiefly al-Adl wal-Ihsan, question the necessity of the monarchy in any form and promote a more conservative social agenda. As long as these different groups fail to coalesce around a coherent and unified set of demands, the monarchy will retain the upper hand.

Looking forwards

Managing a process of gradual reform has been the monarchy's most effective tool in addressing public protest and discontent. In this sense, the king's strategy in 2011 stabilised Morocco at a volatile period and successfully reframed the political debate to focus on the new constitution and strengthening parliamentary powers. Morocco has made significant strides in many areas and shown an ongoing commitment to positive change. What Morocco has failed to do is address broader grievances concerning dignity and socio-economic justice. Progress in these areas is more difficult to measure and could take generations to achieve, even if the political will at the top existed.

The crucial challenge for the monarchy is to avoid discrediting the reform process, either by undermining the elected government, by over-extending the king's executive authority, or harassing its critics excessively. Though the reforms of 2011 did not change the balance of power in Morocco, they were an acknowledgement that there could be limits on the monarchy's authority.

Morocco's record over the last two decades, and since February 2011, demonstrates that widespread public protest can spur the monarchy to accelerate reforms and devolve power. Without addressing deeper issues of inequality, however, opposition will grow, and a future wave of popular uprisings could pose new threats. Then the protests of 1990 and 2011 will not be bookends, but chapters in Morocco's ongoing reform struggle. The next chapter is unlikely to be the last, and future protests could demand more revolutionary, rather than evolutionary, change.

Notes

1 The protests were part of a general strike called by two Moroccan unions. The rioting lasted for several days.

2 Morocco's economic liberalisation policies of the previous decade had taken a toll on the disadvantaged.

3 '33 Dead in 2-Day Riot in Morocco Fed by Frustration Over Economy', Reuters, 17 December 1990, http://www.nytimes.com/1990/12/17/world/33-dead-in-2-day-riot-in-morocco-fed-by-frustration-over-economy.html.

4 Throughout the mid-1990s, Morocco held a number of parliamentary and local elections, and constitutional referendums. A constitutional amendment, passed in 1996, allowed for a directly elected lower house of parliament, a longstanding opposition demand. For a more detailed account of King Hassan II's policies, see Guilain Denoeux and Abdeslam Maghraoui, 'King Hassan's Strategy of Political Dualism', Middle East Policy, vol. 5, no. 4, January 1998, pp. 104–30.

5 According to Human Rights Watch the protests took place 'largely without interference from police, who in some areas were barely in evidence'. See 'Morocco: Thousands March for Reform', Human Rights Watch, 21 February 2011, http://www.hrw.org/news/2011/02/20/morocco-thousands-march-reform.

6 See text of King Mohammed VI's speech, 'King Mohammed VI Speech', 9 March 2011, http://moroccansforchange.com/2011/03/09/king-mohamed-vi-speech-3911-full-text-feb20-khitab/.

7 Morocco is a culturally diverse country with multiple identities: Arab, Islamic, Berber and African. The monarchy binds them together under a broad Moroccan national identity. The common thread through these multiple identities is the strong Islamic foundation of Moroccan society and the king's religious role as commander of the faithful (amir al-mu'minin).

8 See Rom Landau, Moroccan Drama 1900-1950 (San Francisco, CA: The American Academy of Asian Studies, 1956), pp. 36–8.

9 King Mohammed V and the Istiqlal Party, which led Morocco's independence movement, found common cause in independence from France. However, in the ensuing years they competed over setting Morocco's political agenda.

10 The king appointed a constitutional drafting committee headed by Abdellatif Menouni, an adviser to the king. The king also appointed a consultative body to act as a liaison between the committee and a range of political parties, civil-society organisations, labour unions and other constituencies.

11 Morocco's first constitution was adopted in 1962. Subsequent constitutions under Hassan II's reign were issued in 1970, 1972, 1992 and 1996.

12 The National Democratic Institute estimated that up to 25% of ballots in parliamentary elections were either intentionally spoiled in protest or invalidated. The PJD won the largest share of valid votes with close to 23%, almost double

the number for the RNI, the second largest party. See 'Final Report on the Moroccan Legislative Elections', National Democratic Institute, 25 November 2011, https://www.ndi.org/files/Morocco-Final-Election-Report-061812-ENG.pdf.

13 At the end of 1997, Hassan II named Abderrahmane Youssoufi, a longtime leftist political opponent who had spent time in prison and living in exile, as prime minister.

14 In mid-2011 the king established the National Human Rights Council (CNDH), which evolved from the Advisory Council on Human Rights established in the 1990s. The organisation investigates and publicises human-rights issues including prison conditions, migration, child labour and women's rights.

15 This combination of progress and repression has been described as dualism. See Denoeux and Maghraoui, 'King Hassan's Strategy of Political Dualism'.

16 See remarks by Mustafa Elkhalifi in 'Islamists in Power: Views from Within, Building New Regimes After the Uprising', Carnegie Endowment event transcript provided by Federal News Service, Washington DC, 5 April 2012, http://carnegieendowment.org/files/040512_transcript_openingnew-regimes.pdf.

17 The PJD emerged from the Movement of Unity and Reform, a coalition of Islamic movements that competed under the PJD banner in the 1997 parliamentary elections.

18 For an analysis of Moroccan Salafism, see Mohammed Masbah, 'Moving Towards Political Participation: The Moderation of Moroccan Salafis since the Beginning of the Arab Spring', SWP Comments, Comment 01, January 2013, http://www.swp-berlin.org/fileadmin/contents/products/comments/2013C01_msb.pdf.

19 'Morocco King Attends Prayers led by Reformed Salafi-Jihadist', Al Arabiya News, 28 March 2014, http://english.alarabiya.net/en/News/middle-east/2014/03/28/Morocco-king-attends-prayers-led-by-reformed-Salafi-jihadist.html.

20 For a list of early demands and description of the February 20 movement written by movement activists, see Mamfakinch, June 2011, http://pomed.org/wp-content/uploads/2011/06/Press_Kit_June2011.pdf.

21 For a more complete summary of Morocco's economic challenges, see 'Morocco: Selected Issues', *IMF Country Report*, no. 13/110, 18 January 2013, http://www.imf.org/external/pubs/ft/scr/2013/cr13110.pdf.

22 See 'HM The King Delivers Speech to Nation on Occasion of 60th Anniversary of Revolution of King And People', Agence Marocaine de Presse, 20 August 2013, http://www.map.ma/en/activites-royales/hm-king-delivers-speech-nation-occasion-60th-anniversary-revolution-king-and-peopl.

23 In 2005 the palace launched its National Human Development Initiative (INDH) to address the country's dismal socio-economic conditions. The initiative sought to give broader powers to local communities to launch their own development projects to create

jobs, improve housing and address poverty. The programme was coordinated by the Ministry of Interior with a modest annual budget of US$200 million a year. The INDH has undoubtedly helped people, but, after nearly a decade, not enough.

24 See 'Full Text of The Throne Day Speech Delivered By HM King Mohammed VI', Agence Marocaine de Presse, 30 July 2014, http://www.map.ma/en/discours-messages-sm-le-roi/full-text-throne-day-speech-delivered-hm-king-mohammed-vi.

25 See 'Corruption Perceptions Index 2013', Transparency International, http://cpi.transparency.org/cpi2013/results/.

26 See Haim Malka, 'The Struggle for Religious Identity in Tunisia and the Maghreb', Center for Strategic and International Studies, 2 May 2014, http://csis.org/publication/struggle-religious-identity-tunisia-and-maghreb.

27 One of his songs substitutes the word 'freedom' for 'the king' in a national saying: 'God, the nation, and the king'. Al-Haqed has been arrested several times since 2011 on various unrelated charges and subjected to lengthy court proceedings.

28 The king traditionally pardons prisoners every Throne Day (celebrated on 30 July to mark the king's ascension to the throne). One of those pardoned was Daniel Galvan, a Spanish citizen convicted of sexually abusing 11 Moroccan children and sentenced to 30 years in prison.

29 'Protest Culture in Morocco', Economist, 11 June 2014, http://www.economist.com/blogs/pomegranate/2014/06/protest-culture-morocco.

CHAPTER FOUR

Algeria: Enter the Oligarchy

Geoff D. Porter

While political upheaval was developing in the rest of North Africa in 2011, Algerian politics did not grow especially strained until 2013 and 2014. In 2011, protests were limited; significant government spending, including more than US$20 billion in public-sector pay raises, and popular apathy ensured the regime did not face an existential threat. In addition, the state reacted forcefully when the prospect of protests arose. According to one organiser, in February 2011, 35,000 police were deployed to monitor some 2,000 protesters.

But in 2014, President Abdelaziz Bouteflika faced an election for a fourth term in office despite growing health problems, including an extended stay in a Paris hospital in 2013 after reportedly suffering a stroke. He made infrequent appearances, none long and few in which he spoke. Meanwhile, long-standing figures in public service – especially the state's security apparatus – resigned, were dismissed or simply retired. High-level corruption investigations reached a new, but ultimately inconclusive, frenzy. And Algeria's already outspoken press became even more so, with a barbed debate about the country's political future in the run-up to the 2014 presidential election. All of this unfolded amid questions about why Algerians had not rebelled in 2011 and 2012, as had other countries in the region, and whether Algeria would revolt in the future. How sustainable or how vulnerable was Algeria's current political system? Was systemic rupture and political change inevitable in Algeria? Would Bouteflika's re-election mark a turning point towards reform?

Algeria's political system is at best idiosyncratic and at worst unjust. However, it is resilient, because of the distributive nature of the state, primacy of consensus in political decision-making and popular support for a strong security apparatus. Although often over-emphasised, the country's turbulent history during the 1990s has undoubtedly affected the way society interacts with the state; it is seemingly more accepting of an imbalance between security and freedom. In addition, Algerian society has struck something of an informal contract with the state; as long as protests are not violent, refrain from fundamentally challenging the state and focus on local issues, they will be tolerated and protesters' grievances will be largely met.

There are, nonetheless, events that could change this dynamic between state and society. At some point, Bouteflika will die. The timing of his death will be critical for the country's political trajectory. Likewise, the informal social contract could unintentionally be abrogated, prompting Algerians to transform how they interact with the state. It is also possible, but for the moment unlikely, that Algeria could introduce meaningful market reforms. Lastly, there is the so-called fat-tail risk: a low-likelihood, high-impact event, such as the January 2013 In Amenas gas-plant attack, which would scare off much-needed foreign investment.

The 2014 presidential election

In line with expectations, Bouteflika won re-election for his fourth consecutive term in April 2014, with 81.5% of the vote. There was little doubt that Bouteflika would win if he ran, and as long as he was alive, he would run. While sceptics and at least one candidate, Ali Benflis, alleged that the election had been fraudulent, the results were plausible. Bouteflika had secured the support of some large constituent blocs, and although voter-participation rates were low, those who showed up – older urban voters, for example – have historically supported Bouteflika's party, the National Liberation Front (FLN). The election was largely a non-event. Nevertheless, why Bouteflika ran, why he won and what he has done since re-election speak volumes about Algeria's political system.

Le pouvoir

At the root of Algeria's political system is an amorphous group called *le pouvoir* (power), which refers to a network of political and military leaders who control Algeria. The term, however, disguises Algerian politics in opaque exoticness and blurs how the political elite really functions. It may be easier to understand the country's informal political processes as being driven by an oligarchy. The oligarchy consists of those in the top tier of public office (the president, his ministers, the heads of the upper and lower legislatures, and some, but not all, provincial governors), high-ranking officers in the military (both the conventional military and military intelligence), the heads of prominent state-owned enterprises (SOEs), the CEOs of private-sector conglomerates and prominent figures in the business community. The members of the oligarchy largely know and interact with one another outside of their official roles. The network extends to their children as well. Membership in the oligarchy is not fixed nor is one's status within it. Individual fortunes wax and wane depending on shifting influences within the group.

The Algerian oligarchy exerts pressure on formal political institutions to implement policies and enforce regulations that benefit and protect it. Competition within the oligarchy happens through the use of formal levers of the state to get a leg up on rivals or bolster allies. In many ways, Algeria's oligarchy is similar to Russia's, where President Vladimir Putin manages policy and legislation in ways that largely serve to referee disputes between extremely wealthy individuals. Algeria's political system is often characterised as clientelistic, which, while true, does not capture the symbiotic nature of the oligarchy. While public officials do steer benefits to individuals outside government in order to secure their support, those outside government serve important functions for government figures. They offer investment opportunities, create economic space for oligarchs' families and act as a bridge between Algeria and the world for public officials in their private capacities.

Consensus, not coercion

Decisions in Algeria are ultimately made by consensus among the oligarchy. Unlike other governments in the region, there is no decisive power-broker in Algeria capable of acting unilaterally. To be sure, conventional checks and balances on executive power, such as the legislature and judiciary, are weak and the limited autonomy they have from the presidency is not enough to curtail presidential authority.

This does not mean, however, that Bouteflika's power is unfettered. Instead, the constraints under which Bouteflika works are informal, represented by competing clientelistic constituencies. The year prior to the election, for example, was marked by schisms and rivalries among Algeria's political elite jockeying for influence – a situation exacerbated by Bouteflika's lengthy absences from public view. While there were other high-profile political figures who mulled chal-

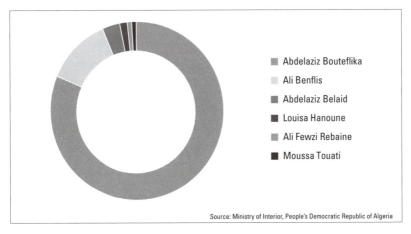

Source: Ministry of Interior, People's Democratic Republic of Algeria

Figure 1. **2014 presidential election results**

lenging Bouteflika's re-election, none could guarantee that the oligarchs would continue to prosper, including those who supported Bouteflika's rivals. In short, had Bouteflika not run or if a more popular, viable candidate had emerged, the patronage network would have been put in jeopardy. Accordingly, different factions within the oligarchy put aside their differences and united behind Bouteflika. Members of *le pouvoir* also opted to postpone fights over how state profits should be divided, in order to ensure their collective profits and state stability would continue.

Popular apathy

Algerians outside of the oligarchy are aware of their marginalisation from the decision-making process. Because they recognise that the oligarchy's sway over legislators and other public officials outweighs any influence they could muster, either individually or collectively, they largely abstain from political participation. The voter participation rate in the presidential election was officially above 50%, but critics claim that it was really 15–18%. It is likely to have been somewhere between the two estimates, which would put it in line with previous participation rates. Some Algerians view their non-participation as a boycott, but for the majority, not voting is simply an acknowledgement of the political reality in which they live.

Protest politics

Instead of engaging in political protests, most Algerians engage in protest politics. An oft-cited figure is that there were more than 10,000 riots, strikes and protests in Algeria in 2013, which, despite a slight increase in the pace and frequency of protests, was a fairly representative year.

Earlier protests, associated with a fledgling movement in 2011, were widely ridiculed and quickly fizzled out. Some of these protests involved thousands of people, as in Ghardaia and Ouargla. Others had no more than a few dozen participants. Despite the discrepancy in size and duration, almost all of the riots, strikes, and protests had localised objectives. Their aim was not to overthrow the political system in Algeria, but to extract more from it. Unrest was about acute social needs – housing, sanitation, water, education, healthcare and salaries from SOEs – that the government could, if pressed, grant.

Protests in Algeria are almost ritualised, with police and protesters alike knowing their roles and recognising the limits of what is acceptable. Local or national politicians then respond to protesters' grievances, by fixing a sewer pipe or running out new electricity lines, for example. But this creates a moral hazard; the successful use of protests to extract concessions, instead of conventional but unresponsive bureaucratic channels, guarantees the continuation of protests. It also encourages protesters to focus on immediate local issues rather than broader criticisms of the state. Protesters know that if they focus on a specific grievance, the state is likely to respond, but if they call for more political rights or freedoms, for example, the state will not offer them anything. Thus, as long as protesters' demands are not grandiose and the state is in a position to meet them, protest politics in Algeria will continue to be a source of regime stability.

Opposition movements

Periodic attempts have sought to form opposition movements that could challenge the oligarchy's political dominance. Several weeks prior to the 2014 presidential election, for example, a movement called 'Barakat' (Enough) emerged, demanding Bouteflika not run for a fourth term. In addition, it claimed that it wanted an end to the 'system'. Barakat, however, stopped short of advancing its own candidate or endorsing one of Bouteflika's opponents in the elections. It also did not articulate how the current system should be dismantled or with what it should be replaced.

In light of its vague and inconclusive message, and its disappearance after the elections, many suspected it to have been an 'astroturf' movement – a group that appeared to be a grassroots movement but was entirely manufactured. After all, the group's inability to put forward a candidate or to propose alternatives to the current system made it an easy foil for *le pouvoir*. The Bouteflika campaign lambasted it for being, at best, ill-conceived and, at worst, misleading the population. On top of that, the campaign said that Barakat's focus on lofty and unrealistic goals showed that it was out of touch with Algeria's day-to-day problems such as housing, employment and the provision of social services. The campaign emphasised that these were the tangible issues that Bouteflika would address.

Signs of sustainability
The distributive state

Although not the sole reason for political stability in Algeria, the economy plays a significant role and hydrocarbons are at its root. In this sense, Algeria is a variant of the classic rentier state: hydrocarbon revenues support the state and pay for the social services that the state offers its citizens. Accordingly, Algeria's hydrocarbons sector ensures the maintenance of Algeria's political elite and their clientelistic relationships. Until the country diversifies its economy, political stability will depend heavily on hydrocarbons output and regional and global energy markets.

After several years of declining output – the impact of which was offset by high, rising oil prices – the domestic hydrocarbons sector may be on the cusp of a revival of production. This will be particularly valuable if lower oil and gas prices since the second half of 2014 persist.

The decline in oil and gas output has been largely due to the failure to bring new fields into production, principally because of three lacklustre oil and gas licensing rounds, as well as acute political infighting that disrupted the sector's commercial operations between 2010 and 2013.

Following a massive shake-up in the hydrocarbons sector, however, Minister of Energy Youcef Yousfi introduced new oil

Figure 2. **Algeria crude oil, condensate and NGLs forecast**

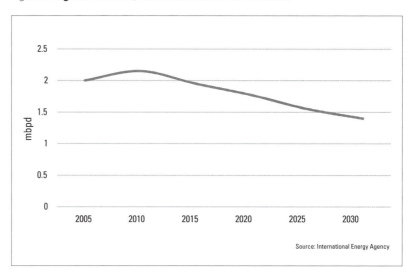

Source: International Energy Agency

and gas licensing terms in January 2013. The new hydrocarbons law removed some of the more onerous terms previously imposed and included incentives for exploiting unconventional oil and gas plays. In addition, Algeria seems keen to acquire enhanced and improved oil recovery technologies that could boost production from existing fields in the immediate term. The blocks awarded in the 2014 licensing round are not likely to begin production until 2018–19, but the renewed interest of international majors in Algeria after almost a decade suggests that the country may finally be on the road to stabilising and then increasing its oil and gas production.

International developments could also work in favour of Algeria's energy sector. In particular, instability in Libya has nearly halted the country's significant hydrocarbons production; Algeria benefitted from higher prices and reduced competition in nearby markets. To be sure, the collapse in global crude prices since June 2014 has significantly curtailed Algeria's hydrocarbon revenues. However, Algeria built up sizeable hard-currency reserves during the boom years. While it has been compelled to shelve some of its more ambitious infrastructure projects, it still has some fiscal manoeuvrability. The shift in Russia-European Union (EU) relations catalysed by events in Ukraine in 2013–14 could also benefit the Algerian economy. Algeria is the third-largest natural-gas exporter to Europe and could benefit from a strategic decision by EU states to cap their reliance on Russian gas.

Domestic and international developments indicate, then, that despite declines in activity and prices in the hydrocarbons sector, Algeria's rentier model could continue. While this would not be a healthy development because it would leave Algeria vulnerable to the vagaries of the commodities market, it would nevertheless allow the country to maintain its political system – protest politics and all.

Support for stability

One of the leading explanations for the absence of an uprising in Algeria in 2011 was that the 1990s' Islamist insurgency was so traumatic that even in the face of profound dissatisfaction with the state, Algerians would not revolt for fear of what could ensue. Although this argument has several flaws, not least that it deprives Algerians of agency and portrays them as victims cowering before memories of their past, it reflects a certain acceptance, if not embrace, by Algerians of a strong security apparatus.

To an extent, the population's reticence to join the regional uprisings in 2011 and 2012 has been validated by the trajectory of revolutions in Libya, Egypt and Syria and Tunisia. As Egypt lurched from revolution to counter-revolution following Muhammad Morsi's brief and heavy-handed presidency, Algerians felt a sense of vicarious déjà vu; the Egyptian situation began to resemble Algeria's own experience following an Islamist electoral victory in 1991. Similarly, the descent into civil war in both Libya and Syria have affirmed Algeria's wariness of dramatic political change and challenging militarily strong regimes. Lastly, although Tunisia has not experienced the same levels of violence as elsewhere in the region, the country's indeterminate political future, as well as an increasing jihadist threat, have convinced Algerians of the merits of incremental political change.

Moreover, the external security threats Algeria has faced since the region's uprisings have produced a 'rally-round-the-flag' effect. The most illustrative example of this was the public response to the catastrophic terrorist attack on the Tigantourine gas facility at In Amenas in January 2013. The attack, claimed by Mokhtar Belmokhtar, a former leader of al-Qaeda in the Islamic Maghreb (AQIM), resulted in the deaths of 39 foreign workers and an Algerian security guard. Although there was

criticism of Algeria's intelligence services for not having antici-
pated and prevented the attack, there was widespread public
support for the military's strong response.

Algerians favour a strong state-security presence in Algiers,
in particular, because of the persistence of AQIM in the
Boumerdes Mountains, several hours' drive southeast of the
capital. AQIM has targeted the capital and continues to carry
out attacks against the military. In addition, the group has
formed ties with a new jihadist organisation in Tunisia – the
Uqba ibn Nafi Brigade – which would give AQIM a new cross-
border dimension. Thus, there is a widespread sense among
Algerians that a strong security apparatus is needed, now and
in the future. To be sure, critics of the government argue that
the military is capable of eradicating AQIM in the Boumerdes
Mountains, but refrains from doing so precisely because the
group's existence justifies maintaining a strong security apparatus.

Algeria is also dealing with a new terrorist threat. In
September 2014, several members of AQIM broke off to form a
group allied to the Islamic State of Iraq and al-Sham (ISIS), Jund
al-Khilafa fi Ard al-Jazair, which then captured and beheaded
a French tourist. Algerian security services claim to have since
largely eradicated the group, but the threat from ISIS members
and supporters in neighbouring Tunisia and Libya remains
high. A number of Algerians have also travelled to Iraq and
Syria to fight either with the Free Syrian Army, the al-Qaeda-
allied Jabhat al-Nusra or ISIS.

Signs of fragmentation
Budgetary constraints
While the state continues to distribute oil rent, in the form of
subsidies and support for under-performing SOEs, in order
to compensate for the lack of political participation, Algerians

have increasingly had to extract concessions from a reluctant government through carefully orchestrated civil unrest.

Part of the state's reluctance to spend freely is due to the Algerian economy's vulnerable position, namely its over-whelming reliance on hydrocarbon revenues. In June 2014, a private-sector lobby, the Forum des Chefs d'Entreprise, held a meeting during which its members emphasised the urgent need to diversify the economy. According to the IMF, global crude prices must be at or above US$121 per barrel for Algeria to fulfil its budgetary obligations; budgeted transfers for subsidies, for example, were 13.6% of GDP in 2012.[1] Currency depreciation, as seen since 2014, will soften the fiscal impact but not eradicate it. Were prices to drop precipitously, Algeria would be likely to maintain its budgetary commitments in the short term, including subsidies on fuel and foodstuffs, by drawing on enormous hard-currency reserves. (Since 2005, when oil prices started their steep upward climb, Algeria has managed to not only pay off almost all of its external debt but also to amass upwards of US$200 billion in currency reserves.) However, were oil prices to remain low for a prolonged period, subsidies would be jeopardised, as would the state's

Figure 3. **Oil price necessary to balance the budget**

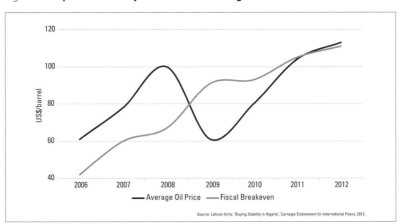

Source: Lahcen Achy, 'Buying Stability in Algeria', Carnegie Endowment for International Peace, 2013.

ability to respond to social unrest and long-practised clientelism.

An expanding oligarchy

In addition to an increased budget, the size of Algeria's oligarchy is expanding, as are the number of privileges demanded from the state. For example, in the final weeks before the presidential election, Bouteflika made amends with powerful politicians with whom he had fallen out. These included two of his former prime ministers, Abdelaziz Belkhadem and Ahmed Ouyahia. Belkhadem had been ousted from the FLN leadership during Bouteflika's tenure and Ouyahia had been unceremoniously dumped as prime minister in 2012. Having then supported Bouteflika's campaign, Belkhadem and Ouyahia expect to be compensated following his re-election.

Either what is available to oligarchs must increase through economic growth or the number of people making demands must be reduced. The oligarchy may, of course, opt for a combination – making the pie bigger *and* letting fewer people claim slices.

What lies ahead

Several questions will determine Algeria's future: whether the country will embrace wide-reaching economic reforms; whether the state will make a grave misstep, triggering an unpredictable response from the public; whether a black-swan event, similar to the In Amenas gas-plant attack, will occur; and the state of Bouteflika's health – whether he will be able to continue leading the country.

An Algerian infitah

How likely is an Algerian economic opening? The country has tremendous potential and needs, something that foreign investors have long recognised but have been at pains to take advantage of. Manufacturing costs are low, labour is abundant and the consumer market is virtually untapped. However, privatisation of SOEs will proceed only if the current generation of political leadership guarantees for itself and its progeny privileged access to those privatised state assets and immunity against possible corruption charges. As the leadership ages and tries to transfer control to a younger generation, there could then be privatisation akin to what occurred under Anwar Sadat's *infitah* (openness) policy in Egypt in the mid-1970s or to Boris Yeltsin's hasty privatisation of SOEs in Russia in the early 1990s. Although no current government official is openly advocating rapid privatisation, other members of the oligarchy have hinted at it, including members of the powerful Forum des Chefs d'Entreprise, as well as former members of government. If an Algerian *infitah* were to occur, alongside a rebound in the oil and gas sectors, the country could experience the economic renaissance that has eluded it for so long.

A grave misstep

Despite cautious planning and the orchestrated waltz between the regime and protesters, mistakes can happen. In 2001, just such a misstep occurred, with the death of a young man while in police custody. The events that followed became known as the Black Spring and resulted in enormous pressure on the government, which was forced to make concessions to the Berber community to which the prisoner belonged. Were an event similar to the Black Spring to transpire, it would be difficult for the state to quickly regain its footing, potentially triggering wide-scale unrest. Whether this unrest would translate into calls to dismantle the current political system or simply the dismissal of key political figures is uncertain. A mistake would be viewed as the state violating the established norms of protest politics, thus allowing protesters to transgress those norms as well.

Protests in the southern Algerian town of In Salah regarding potential shale-gas exploitation, in particular, pose a challenge. Algiers needs the revenue that such exploitation could yield; thus it is unlikely to capitulate to demands that the state impose a ban on shale-gas exploitation across the country. However, the state will have to offer protesters something if it wants to bring an end to the demonstrations. It must be wary to avoid a misstep that could spark off wider condemnation of its actions.

Bouteflika's tenure

The question of how much longer Bouteflika will live has dominated Algerian political commentary for the past six years. Aged 77 and in poor health, the president has been counted out numerous times, but has proved to be resilient. At some point, though, he will die or be considered unfit to continue. Political decision-makers would then be likely to emphasise the need to maintain order and ensure a stable transition. Constitutional processes would then be followed; the president of the upper house of Algeria's legislature would assume the presidency on a provisional basis and organise an election 90 days later.

The challenge for Algeria's oligarchy to reach a consensus on a candidate to support for the first post-Bouteflika election. Arguably, the main reason Bouteflika was re-elected was precisely because the political elite could not decide on any other candidate. If Bouteflika were to die in his fourth term, Yousfi, or Prime Minister Abdelmalek Sellal could be backed as presidential candidates, but this would only be likely in the short term.

Contention over who succeeds Bouteflika probably became less heated following the departure in September 2015 of Algeria's long-standing intelligence chief, Gen. Mohamed

'Tewfik' Mediène, thought to be one of the main obstacles to a consensus candidate. However, Tewfik's sudden resignation seemingly cleared the path for a smoother succession scenario. But it remains to be seen whether Tewfik is genuinely no longer as influential as he once was or if his influence has become even more clandestine now that he does not hold an official position.

A black swan

Large-scale terrorist attacks could alter Algeria's current trajectory. There is precedent: the catastrophic In Amenas attack took the Algerian intelligence community entirely by surprise. The fact that Algeria's renowned intelligence services missed the warning signs suggests they may not be able to prevent a similar attack in the future.

Moreover, terrorist groups are increasingly active in the region. Belmokhtar exploited poor security and surveillance in southwestern Libya and it is believed that his organisation, al-Mourabitoun, and possibly AQIM, have established training camps in southern Libya. The emergence of the al-Qaeda-allied Uqba ibn Nafi Brigade in Tunisia is also concerning. In 2014, the group attacked Tunisian security services in Jebel ech Chambi, killing at least 14 Tunisian soldiers.[2] Another growing threat is ISIS, which is now well established in Libya and seems to be making inroads in Tunisia. Lastly, despite a French military intervention in January 2013, terrorist groups remain active in northern Mali, including groups associated with Belmokhtar, AQIM, and an AQIM splinter group called the Movement for Unity and Jihad in West Africa (MUJAO). A suicide bomber linked to al-Mourabitoun killed a French soldier in Gao in July 2014.

For now, Algerians have given up freedoms in exchange for security promised by the state. To endanger regime stability, though, a terrorist attack would have to fundamentally change how this informal contract was viewed. If the state appeared no longer able to guarantee public safety, Algerians might reevaluate their support for the regime.

Conclusion

Algeria's political leadership and oligarchy are not blind to how the system works or the challenges it faces. For the moment, the leadership will be likely to maintain the status quo. Barring unforeseen events – such as Bouteflika's death, a misstep by the state, rapid privatisation or a sustained terrorist campaign – Algerians will probably continue to try to find ways to either game and extract more from the system, or leave Algeria altogether. They recognise that there is little likelihood that anyone outside of the political elite will lead the country and there is no viable model to replace the current system even if it were overthrown. Thus, Algerians may not be happy with their current circumstances but have mostly come to accept them.

Notes

[1] 'Algeria: Selected Issues', *IMF Country Report*, no. 14/34, February 2014, http://www.imf.org/external/pubs/ft/scr/2014/cr1434.pdf.

[2] Tarek Amara, 'Militants Kill 14 Tunisian Soldiers in Mountain Ambush', Reuters, 17 July 2014, http://news.yahoo.com/tunisia-says-death-toll-militant-attack-rises-14-073914040.html.

CHAPTER FIVE

Jihadism in North Africa: A House of Many Mansions

Jean-Pierre Filiu

A common narrative links the recent developments of the jihadist scene in North Africa to the toppling of the Tunisian and Libyan dictatorships and their tightly controlled security apparatuses. This narrative drives the propaganda of the remaining strongmen in the region, who portray themselves as the best antidote to al-Qaeda in particular, and terrorism in general. Western intelligence, overwhelmingly critical of NATO's anti-Gadhafi campaign, also tends to share this view, preferring stability and thus placing their trust in collaborative authoritarian regimes.

The main flaw of this 'counter-revolutionary' narrative is its lack of historical perspective. The whole story of jihadism in North Africa started two decades ago, when the Algerian army 'suspended' the electoral process in 1992 that would have brought the local Islamists to power, precipitating a horrendous civil war. Understanding the roots and mutations of Algerian jihadism reveals how a complex and volatile situation has coalesced today around competing poles and networks.

Its history begins in Algeria, which became the cradle of an enduring version of jihadism that expanded through the Sahara in the form of al-Qaeda in the Islamic Maghreb (AQIM), before being rolled back from Mauritania. It continues with the birth and growth of a new brand of jihadist outfit, Ansar al-Sharia, in the aftermath of the Tunisian and Libyan revolutions. The third section addresses the rise and fall of the AQIM-linked 'Jihadistan' in Northern Mali, with the recent development of an ambitious movement, al-Mourabitoun, led by an Algerian veteran. It concludes with a discussion of the Islamic State of Iraq and al-Sham (ISIS) and its implications for global and regional jihadism.

Algeria's jihadists and Mauritania's roll-back

The Islamic Armed Group (GIA) was the main jihadist organisation fighting the Algerian regime in the 1990s.[1] As the civil war dragged on, the GIA also intensified its struggle against the rival Islamic Salvation Front (FIS). Although they were often nicknamed 'Afghans' because of their Salafist attire, only a small minority of the Algerian jihadists actually fought in Afghanistan against Soviet forces (before their withdrawal in 1989). Among those veterans was Mokhtar Belmokhtar, or Belaouar, 'the one-eyed man' (he reportedly lost an eye while fighting in the Afghan province of Khost in 1991).

Belmokhtar, born in the oasis of Ghardaia, was based in the Algerian Sahara, where he handled various logistics operations for the GIA. A shrewd smuggler himself, Belmokhtar built over several years an intricate network of criminal partnerships in the Sahel region.[2] Soon he was nicknamed 'Mister Marlboro' for his trafficking of tobacco, though he also smuggled drugs and arms. Such 'un-Islamic' dealings were either ignored or justified by an obligation to defeat the *kuffâr* (infidels) by any means necessary.

On the eastern border with Libya, a much smaller smuggling network operated on behalf of the GIA. One of its main ringleaders was Abdelhamid Abou Zeid, who boasted of dealing only in computers and tea, in order to enhance his pious credentials. Neither Belmokhtar nor Abou Zeid engaged in insurgency activities then. But they eventually joined the Salafist Group for Preaching and Combat (GSPC) in 1998 when it broke away from a GIA responsible for a wave of mass killings and plagued by internal purges.

The collapse of the GIA led the Algerian military to proclaim victory, while acknowledging there remained 'residual terrorism', mostly in the mountainous range of Kabylia, east of the capital Algiers. Abou Zeid rose in the hierarchy of the GSPC but operated mostly in its smuggling underworld. Belmokhtar, by contrast, sought to emphasise his leadership capacities, naming the *katiba* (battalion) of his supporters 'al-Moulathamoun', the Veiled Ones, with reference to warring tribes who had spread Islam in the Sahara.

In 2004, both Belmokhtar and Abou Zeid pledged allegiance to the new GSPC emir, Abdelmalek Droukdel, who had joined the jihadi insurgency at the same time as them and had managed to escape military raids and purges. Droukdel strove to globalise the GSPC network by connecting it to the anti-US jihad in Iraq. GSPC training camps in eastern Algeria attracted hundreds of militants from all over North Africa, eager to fight against the 'Crusaders' in the Middle East.[3]

In 2005, Belmokhtar declared jihad against Mauritania, attacking an isolated outpost and slaughtering its whole garrison. He felt the need to boost his jihadist profile against an enemy that lacked the resources to strike back. This escalation led Belmokhtar to endorse Droukdel's pledge of allegiance to Osama bin Laden, issued on the fifth anniversary of the 9/11 attacks.

In January 2007, the GSPC officially became al-Qaeda in the Islamic Maghreb (AQIM). The Algerian capital was struck by deadly suicide attacks in April and December that year. But AQIM failed to export its terror north of the Mediterranean, where it had no solid network or pool of supporters. So Droukdel turned to Belmokhtar in order to achieve AQIM's global ambitions. In the last days of 2007, Belmokhtar's affiliates killed four French tourists in eastern Mauritania, and the Paris–Dakar car race was consequently moved to Latin America.

After years of restraint, Abou Zeid also escalated attacks. He initiated a chase for Western hostages all over the Sahara, compelling Belmokhtar to join the fray. The extremely mobile commandos struck from the coast of Mauritania to Southern Tunisia. The abductions brought unprecedented media exposure to the two jihadist leaders, along with hefty ransoms that further extended their reach and influence.

Mauritania was hit repeatedly, even in the capital, Nouakchott. It took three years for the local army to gather the military and intelligence capabilities to launch a fully fledged offensive against AQIM. But in 2008–09, the organisation was rolled back from Mauritanian territory. That the Mauritanian state proclaimed its own jihad against those claiming to represent jihadists contributed significantly to the success of this campaign.

Conversely, in Mali the failure of a military operation in July 2009 led to the local army's de facto abandonment of the north, limiting its control to the cities of Timbuktu, Gao and Kidal. Northern Mali became a safe haven for both Belmokhtar and Abou Zeid. Algerian cadres still formed the top leadership of AQIM, even in the Sahara, which convinced African jihadists to form their own outfit, the Movement for Unity and Jihad in West Africa (MUJAO).

On the eve of the Tunisian revolution, Droukdel had become dependent on his subordinates in the Sahara. They supplied him with the financial resources and media exposure he badly needed in his isolated stronghold of Kabylia. Mauritania had successfully liberated its territory from AQIM and often undertook raids in neighbouring Mali. In Algeria, outbursts of residual terrorism occurred, but without affecting the political scene.

The Tunisian and Libyan revolutions

AQIM remained quiet during the Tunisian uprising that ousted President Ben Ali in January 2011, ending 23 years of his dictatorship.[4] In the euphoria of the revolution, all political detainees were unconditionally released. One was particularly problematic. Seifallah Benhassine, nicknamed 'Abou Iyad al-Tounissi' (the Tunisian), was not a prisoner of conscience but the former leader of the Tunisian guest house in the radical community in Peshawar during anti-Soviet jihad.

Abou Iyad became a key leader of the Islamic Tunisian Fighting Group (GICT), a partner of al-Qaeda, whose leadership he interacted with frequently. In 2003, during one of his liaison missions in Turkey, he was arrested by the local police and extradited to Tunisia. He was condemned to 63 years in jail for terrorist activities, including masterminding the killing of Ahmed Shah Massoud, the Afghan commander of the anti-Taliban resistance, two days before 9/11.

The revolution also prompted the return from exile of Rached Ghannouchi and the legalisation of his Islamist Ennahda (Renaissance) Party. The Islamist movement had been plagued by years of repression that had deepened a generational divide between the historic leadership, now released from jails or back from exile, and younger grassroots militants. Ennahda, despite its roots in the Muslim Brotherhood, had grown into a catch-all Islamist party that also included significant representation from Tunisia's Salafists.

The post-revolutionary Tunisian landscape was therefore quite different from the Egyptian one, where a fully-fledged

Salafist party had developed independently of the Muslim Brotherhood. Ennahda, however, sought to absorb and moderate most of the Salafist militants. This would be crucial in the coming debates about the Tunisian Second Republic, whose constitution would replace the founding charter adopted after the end of the French protectorate in 1956.

Ennahda won 36% of the votes, but received 89 out of 217 seats in the October 2011 elections for the Constituent Assembly. It entered into a coalition with a socialist party and a nationalist one to form a tripartite government chaired by Hamadi Jebali, Ennahda's secretary-general. Throughout this period, Ghannouchi kept cajoling the Salafist 'brothers' in an effort to win over their networks instead of suppressing or marginalising them.

This tolerance substantially helped Abou Iyad expand his own organisation, which he named Ansar al-Sharia. Jebali and his minister of interior, Ali Laarayedh, silently disapproved of Ghannouchi's lenient stance, but ultimately endured provocations by Ansar al-Sharia. The secular opposition criticised Ennahda's double standard, accusing the Islamist-led government of playing with jihadi fire.

In contrast to the relatively peaceful revolution in Tunisia, the struggle against Gadhafi's regime in Libya quickly became a full-blown civil war that lasted from February to October 2011. Dissidents from the government army joined forces in the insurgency with jihadist veterans of the Libyan Islamic Fighting Group (LIFG).[5] In 2007, the LIFG had split between a Pakistan-based nucleus that merged into al-Qaeda, including Abu Anas al-Libi, and its Libyan members who eventually rejected bin Laden's mentorship and jihadist dogma in 2010.[6]

After Gadhafi's fall, the leader of this 'reformed' LIFG, Abdelhakim Belhaj,[7] moved to Tripoli. He became the new military governor and founded a political party, al-Watan

(The Motherland). Meanwhile, in Benghazi, the cradle of the Libyan revolution, Muhammad al-Zahawi developed his own Ansar al-Sharia. Zahawi, like Abou Iyad, had been previously imprisoned. But he had never fought outside Libya, let alone in Afghanistan. There was no organisational or operational link between the Tunisian and Libyan Ansar al-Sharia groups, just a shared motivation to defy the paths chosen by the legalised Islamist or reformed jihadist parties.

In another contrast with the Tunisian revolution, Libyan Islamists fared poorly at the first elections; in July 2012, the local branch of the Muslim Brotherhood, running as the Justice and Construction Party (JCP), won only 17 out of 80 party seats in the General National Congress (GNC); 120 seats of the 200-member GNC were allotted to individuals not affiliated with any party. But the JCP was much better structured than its rival organisations and soon gained the loyalty of a sizeable number of 'independent' members of the Congress.

Belhaj's Watan Party received less than 4% of the votes in the same contest. Nevertheless, he remained the only leader to play a significant role in both parliament and on the streets of Tripoli. The revolutionary militias (*thuwar*) continued to be the main source of power in the major cities.

In September 2012, the dissemination on the internet of a video slandering the Prophet Muhammad was seized as a pretext by extremist groups to stir violent protests against US embassies and consulates in the region. On the 11th anniversary of 9/11, the US consulate in Benghazi came under attack and the United States' ambassador was killed, along with three of his compatriots. The Obama administration held Ansar al-Sharia responsible, suggesting an al-Qaeda connection to the attacks.

However, it appeared that local militia leaders, already responsible for summary executions of 'traitors' (revolutionary renegades from Gadhafi's regime involved in earlier anti-Islamist crackdowns), had launched the deadly attack.[8] US intelligence, focused on global threats, had underestimated the dangers of Benghazi warlords. In June 2014, the US captured a key suspect involved in the attacks, Ahmed Abu Khattala, and transported him to New York to face trial.

In Tunisia, there was no doubt that Ansar al-Sharia led an assault on the US Embassy in Tunis on 14 September 2012. The presidential guard had to intervene, killing five protesters. Abou Iyad staged a last defiant rally in a mosque in central Tunis before going underground. Jebali and Laarayedh had finally prevailed against Ghannouchi in imposing a tough line against Ansar al-Sharia. The Islamist-led government even let two Ansar al-Sharia hunger-strikers die in jail, rejecting their demands.

Then, in February 2013, Chokri Belaïd, a prominent leftist leader, was shot dead next to his home in Tunis. The murder was blamed on a Salafist death squad, but the political crisis, with a general strike and mass protests in the capital, led to the downfall of the Jebali government. Jebali tried to form a new technocratic cabinet without party representation, but Ghannouchi refused any devolution of power by Ennahda.

Eventually, the former minister of interior, Ali Laarayedh, became prime minister and pursued a showdown with Ansar al-Sharia. The group's annual conference in the city of Kairouan was banned and ensuing riots were supressed. The Tunisian public overwhelmingly supported this 'iron fist' policy, since Ansar al-Sharia had been accused of killing yet another prominent leftist activist. For months, the security forces hunted down Ansar al-Sharia militants, eventually killing some of their armed hardliners.

But another shadow was looming on the horizon of the Tunisian revolution; AQIM, after repeated infiltrations, had managed in June 2013 to consolidate a base in the Jebel Chambi, a mountainous range on the border with Algeria. Skirmishes and improvised explosive devices (IEDs) inflicted an unprecedented toll on the Tunisian military and police, who in turn protested against the Islamist-led government. The jihadist stronghold was eventually neutralised, although escape routes to Algeria did not allow the poorly equipped Tunisian forces to eliminate the threat once and for all.

Again, Algeria appeared to be the source of the jihadist spillover into neighbouring countries. The incapacity of post-Gadhafi Libya to disarm the militias had also created fertile ground for cooperation between warlords, jihadists and smugglers. This created serious security concerns in southern Tunisia.[9]

In October 2013, US special forces captured Abou Anas al-Libi outside his Tripoli home. Abou Anas was a Libyan al-Qaeda associate wanted for the 1998 bombing of US embassies in Kenya and Tanzania, who had returned to his native country after Gadhafi's fall. But his capture aggravated the power struggle in Libya, prompting the brief abduction of the prime minister himself by a militia that accused him of complicity with the CIA.[10]

In January 2014, three years after the Tunisian revolution, a new constitution was finally adopted and Ennahda relinquished the presidency, opening the way for a technocratic cabinet. This globally recognised success proved to be the best antidote to jihadist destabilisation for more than a year. But in March 2015, two jihadist commandos attacked the Bardo National Museum, in the same grounds as the Tunisian parliament. They killed more than 20 people before being gunned down by local security. Just three months later, a lone Tunisian gunman attacked tourists at a beach resort in Sousse, killing 39 people.

All three Tunisian terrorists had been trained in neighbouring Libya, where the fight between the Tripoli-based Dawn coalition and its Tobruk-based Dignity alliance degenerated into a full-fledged civil war in 2014, with direct Egyptian and Emirati support on behalf of Dignity and long-stalled efforts by the United Nations (UN) to broker a national unity agreement. Dignity brands all its opponents as terrorists, while Dawn accuses former Gadhafi supporters of not being sufficiently committed to the revolution. Despite these mutual accusations, both Tripoli and Tobruk have been targeted by jihadist attacks. The political impasse, decline in governance and widespread warlordism has made Libya the most fertile ground for jihadism in North Africa, even allowing ISIS to take root in 2015.

The Mali Campaign and the rise of al-Mourabitoun

As the Arab uprisings were about to unfold, the two AQIM leaders in the Sahara, Belmokhtar and Abou Zeid, found safe havens in Northern Mali to pursue their own criminal activities and jihadist operations. In September 2010, Abou Zeid led an attack on the French expatriate compound in Arlit, a uranium facility in northern Mali. Seven hostages were abducted; three of them were released after several months, while the other four, all French nationals, were held captive for three years.

The complex negotiations on the fate of foreign hostages absorbed a lot of the attention of the two leaders. Belmokhtar relied on a mediator close to the president of Burkina Faso. But Abou Zeid favoured the intercession of Iyad Ag Ghali, a former guerrilla leader of the Touareg insurgency in northern Mali, who had returned home after a term as consul of Mali in the Saudi port city of Jeddah.

Touaregs have a long history of armed uprisings against the central government in Bamako since their first rebellion in 1963. Iyad Ag Ghali, a partner in the most recent peace agreement with the Malian authorities (who rewarded him with the Jeddah consular assignment), with increasing frequency denounced the failure of Bamako to live up to its commitments to the Touaregs. But his association with Abou Zeid led him to adopt a sharply Islamist tone, eventually founding a new group, Ansar Eddine (Supporters of Religion).

Thousands of Malian Touaregs, including veteran anti-Bamako guerrillas, found refuge in Libya and joined Gadhafi's mercenary units known as the Islamic Legion. When the Libyan dictatorship collapsed in the autumn of 2011, the Legion disbanded and the Touareg fighters moved back to Mali, along with weaponry seized from Gadhafi's caches. Most of them joined Ansar Eddine, empowering Iyad Ag Ghali with unprecedented force.

In January 2012, Ansar Eddine allied with the Touareg separatist insurgency, the National Movement for the Liberation of Azawad (MNLA), Azawad being the Touareg denomination for northern Mali. Ansar Eddine and the MNLA took over the cities of Kidal, Timbuktu and Gao in a matter of weeks. A military coup in Bamako only accelerated the demise of the central government in the north of the country.

The MNLA proclaimed the independence of Azawad in March. But its victory was short lived, because Ansar Eddine, backed by AQIM and the MUJAO, turned against its former allies to consolidate full jihadist control of northern Mali. Each of the jihadist groups had its own fiefdom: Ansar Eddine in Kidal, AQIM in Timbuktu and the MUJAO in Gao. Belmokhtar had been marginalised by the close cooperation between Abou Zeid and Iyad Ag Ghali.

Abou Zeid delivered the final blow to his Algerian rival in November by convincing Droukdel to expel Belmokhtar from AQIM. The charges against him ranged from embezzlement of hostage ransoms to a poor record in jihadist activism. A defiant

Belmokhtar chose to spend more time in southern Libya, where he benefitted from the local anarchy of the post-Gadhafi power vacuum.

Algeria bet on the peace talks it had sponsored between Ansar Eddine and the Malian government. The Algerian military was therefore incensed when Ansar Eddine and its jihadist allies launched an offensive towards the south of Mali in January 2013, occupying the strategic town of Konna. Bamako called Paris for help because the road to the capital was now open to jihadist commandos.

The French response, known as *Operation Serval*, was swift and on a large scale. Algerian airspace was opened to the French air force, a dramatic move that underlined the shared concern about the jihadist threat. The UN, African Union and European Union endorsed the campaign and relied on US and British support with logistics and intelligence. Chadian commandos were also crucial in the ground operation.

In six weeks, the French military managed to stop the jihadist push and roll back their units, before liberating the cities of Gao, Timbuktu and Kidal. A merciless offensive in the extreme northeast of the country, in the Ametetai valley, successfully destroyed the jihadist stronghold there. French sources estimated that 700 out of 2,000 jihadist fighters died in combat,[11] and Abou Zeid was killed while trying to flee. The 'Jihadistan' that AQIM, Ansar Eddine and the MUJAO had established in northern Mali lasted less than a year. While no weapons NATO had delivered to the Libyan insurgents in 2011 were found in jihadist caches, they were replete with arms plundered from Gadhafi's arsenals.

As his former partners were being routed in Mali, Belmokhtar masterminded a major terror attack that returned him to the centre of the jihadist scene. In January 2013, the oil complex of In Amenas in southern Algeria was taken over by commandos comprising Belmokhtar's supporters. The Algerian military eventually recaptured the facilities, but 40 hostages from ten countries were killed, along with 29 terrorists.[12]

Belmokhtar took credit for the operation, pushing both Droukdel and Abou Zeid into the shadows. The killing of Abou Zeid and dismantling of AQIM's safe haven in Mali further served Belmokhtar's plans to become the undisputed jihadist leader of the entire Sahara region. Southern Libya, in particular, offered unrivalled opportunities for the war-hardened survivor and seasoned smuggler.

In May 2013, the MUJAO proved it had outlived AQIM by launching combined suicide attacks against military targets in Niger, including the city of Arlit. In August, Belmokhtar's group and the MUJAO announced their merger into a new organisation, al-Mourabitoun, a name that reflected the celebrated fighters who spread Islam in the Sahara in the 11th century.

Did the French-led campaign simply displace the jihadist menace from northern Mali to southern Libya? Belmokhtar and al-Mourabitoun may have found a new safe haven in southern Libya, but they are only one group in an area complicated by rivalries between the ethnic-Tubu, Arab and Touareg tribes and feuds between revolutionaries and those nostalgic for the toppled dictatorship.

What made the prospect of a Malian 'Jihadistan' so dangerous was the process of association, and then identification, between Touareg irredentists and jihadists, similar to how Pashtun nationalists in Afghanistan and Pakistan progressively blended with jihadist activists. Such a 'Talibanisation' process would have been devastating for the whole region, because sizeable Touareg communities exist not only in Mali and Libya, but also in Niger and Algeria.

Operation Serval was therefore not purely a military success. The French move paved the way for the rapid restoration of Malian institutions, with general elections for the presidency in August 2013 and parliament in November. The new head of state, Ibrahim Boubacar Keïta, won 77% of the votes. Significantly, he brought the former number two and three of Ansar Eddine into his presidential party. Although a new national pact has yet to bind northern Mali to the rest of the country, Keïta has the potential and mandate to draft and implement such a pact.

The new global appeal of the Middle East

The impact of Western military interventions in Libya and Mali are still difficult to evaluate. The NATO campaign against the Libyan dictatorship certainly prevented a wave of violence had Gadhafi defeated the rebels and been restored to absolute power. Jihadists could have also played a bigger role in the insurgency, especially in Cyrenaica (eastern Libya), in the absence of Western interference.

Nevertheless, NATO lacked the will to ensure a stabilised post-Gadhafi Libya. And, despite its dramatic success in dismantling the AQIM stronghold, the French intervention in Mali will depend on a reconciliation process between the central power in Bamako and Touareg activists. If mediation is required, it has to be regional, and most probably Algerian – definitely not Western.

Despite an aggressive campaign on jihadist websites, the French-led operation in Mali attracted very few volunteers from abroad – in sharp contrast to the Syrian war, which became a magnet for North African militants. Libyans and Tunisians rank among the top nationalities of foreign fighters in Syria, along with Saudis and Iraqis.[13] Abu Bakr al-Baghdadi, ISIS' leader, has openly challenged Ayman Zawahiri, bin Laden's official successor, for the supreme position in the globalised jihad.[14] In this merciless feud, most North African jihadists have tried to remain neutral, though this neutrality is already a blow to Zawahiri's leadership.[15] Maghrebi jihadists and volunteer fighters have more often supported ISIS, raising concerns among North African governments over how to manage these fighters when they return home.

In conjunction with its expansion in Syria and Iraq, ISIS began to establish a foothold in the Libyan city of Derna in November 2014. Local supporters of al-Baghdadi attempted to create a base of operations where other radical factions had long resisted Ghadafi's rule. But this proved to be a failed tactic. After ISIS assassinated a local jihadist commander in June 2015, its fighters were defeated in Derna. However, ISIS regrouped and seized the central city of Sirte, Gadhafi's hometown, which had previously been under the control of militias from Misrata. The ongoing Libyan civil war between the Tobruk-based House of Representatives and the Tripoli-based GNC and their affiliated militias exacerbated the growth of jihadism because each side prioritised defeating the other over combatting the spread of ISIS.

The ensuing power struggle for the leadership of the global jihad between Zawahiri and Baghdadi will be a major component of jihadism in North Africa in the future. National contexts and factional feuds will also complicate the jihadist equation. One sure thing is that jihadism in North Africa will remain 'a house of many mansions', divided primarily between the rising influence of ISIS-affiliated factions, remaining AQIM members and opportunistic elements of al-Mourabitoun.

Notes

1   The best study on that period is Luis Martinez, *The Algerian civil war 1990-98* (London: Hurst, 2000), especially Chapter Four.

2   Jean-Baptiste Rivoire and Salima Mellah, 'Enquête sur l'étrange "Ben Laden" du Sahara', *Le Monde Diplomatique*, February 2005.

3 Jean-Pierre Filiu, 'The local and global jihad of Al-Qa'eda in the Islamic Maghrib', *Middle East Journal*, vol. 63, no. 2, Spring 2009, pp. 220–3.

4 Jean-Pierre Filiu, *The Arab Revolution: Ten Lessons from the Democratic Uprising* (London: Hurst, 2011), p. 108.

5 Luis Martinez, *The Libyan paradox* (New York: Columbia University Press, 2007), pp. 70–1.

6 ILFG, *Al-Murajaat* (The Revisions), Cairo, Madbouli, 2010.

7 See Isabelle Mandraud, *Du Djihad aux Urnes* (Paris: Stock, 2013), pp. 153–8.

8 David Kirkpatrick, 'A Deadly mix in Benghazi', *New York Times*, 28 December 2013, http://www.nytimes.com/projects/2013/benghazi/#/?chapt=0.

9 International Crisis Group, 'Tunisia's Borders: Jihadism and Contraband', *Middle East and North Africa Report*, no. 148, 28 November 2013.

10 Isabelle Mandraud, 'L'exécutif libyen menacé par les luttes de pouvoir', *Le Monde*, 11 October 2013, http://www.lemonde.fr/afrique/article/2013/10/11/l-executif-libyen-menace-par-la-lutte-des-pouvoirs_3494086_3212.html.

11 Alexandra Geneste and Nathalie Guibert, 'La France organise, aux Nations Unies, son retrait militaire du Mali', *Le Monde*, 27 April 2013, http://www.lemonde.fr/international/article/2013/04/26/la-france-organise-aux-nations-unies-son-retrait-militaire-du-mali_3167223_3210.html.

12 See Statoil, 'The In-Amenas Attack', presented to the Board of Directors on 11 September 2013, http://www.statoil.com/en/NewsAndMedia/News/2013/Pages/12Sep_InAmenas_report.aspx.

13 See Aaron Zelin, Evan Kohlmann and Laith al-Khouri, 'Convoy of Martyrs in the Levant', Washington Institute for Near East Policy, June 2013, http://www.washingtoninstitute.org/uploads/Documents/opeds/Zelin20130601-FlashpointReport-v2.pdf.

14 Jean-Pierre Filiu, 'Al-Qaeda is Dead, Long Live Al-Qaeda', Carnegie International Endowment for Peace, 22 April 2014, http://carnegieendowment.org/syriaincrisis/?fa=55401.

15 Nelly Lahoud and Muhammad al-Ubaydi, 'The War of Jihadis Against Jihadis in Syria', *CTC Sentinel*, March 2014, vol. 7, no. 3, p. 5.

CHAPTER SIX

A New Economic Model for North Africa

Svetlana Milbert

Four years after the Arab uprisings swept through the Middle East and North Africa (MENA) and toppled leaders who had ruled for decades in Egypt, Libya, Tunisia and Yemen, countries in the region continue to undergo a transition to address socio-economic and political grievances. Several of the uprisings in North Africa produced political changes but have yet to foster the kind of economic conditions demonstrators demanded when they took to the streets in late 2010 and 2011. They called primarily for jobs, a reduction in poverty and inequality, and access to opportunities. To placate their restive populations, North African governments have applied a mix of populist and reform policies, as a temporary stopgap to prevent more instability while they sort out a new political arrangement. Governments and dominant political classes have prioritised political stability over adopting economic policies that will be painful in the short term but necessary to create jobs and fuel growth in the long term. Despite the momentum of change, politics is closely intertwined with the potential for meaningful economic reform. Whether the new or existing governments in the region have the fortitude to take on the vested interests of privileged classes and the ingenuity to gain the support of the population will go a long way in determining the future trajectory of North Africa.

Economic performance before the uprisings

During 2000–10, North African countries grew at a steady pace, averaging nearly 4.5% of GDP, while inflation was contained to a low average of 2% of GDP (Table 1). Despite apparent sound macroeconomic performance, however, unemployment rates remained high and growth was not shared by all segments of the population. For years, state resources were transferred through an expansive system of subsidies, as a deliberate political measure to appease the masses by keeping prices artificially low on staple goods. Governments undertook limited economic reforms, resembling a neoliberal framework, as a way to improve macroeconomic performance and facilitate greater trade and investment.[1] However, enclosed political systems and entrenched interests fostered crony capitalism and led to rampant corruption. A 2014 study by the World Bank examining Tunisia's economy under President Zine al-Abidine Ben Ali found that policies and regulations were deliberately tailored to benefit and protect the economic interests of the privileged members of the ruling family and their affiliates.[2] As large segments of the population were perpetually isolated from economic opportunity, they grew restless and resentful of ruling regimes, culminating in widespread protests in Egypt, Tunisia, Libya, Yemen and Bahrain.

In the decade prior to the January 2011 uprising that ousted Ben Ali, Tunisia was growing at an average yearly rate of 4.4%, but a mounting budget deficit and slowdown in revenues left the country financially vulnerable and unable to address rising unemployment and inequality. The Ben Ali regime also manipulated economic policies and regulations to benefit family

Table 1. **North Africa: Macroeconomic indicators, 2000–10 average (percentage change)**

	GDP growth	Inflation	Fiscal balance	Current-account balance
Algeria	3.9	3.3	-0.4	14.5
Libya	4.6	0.3	12.6	25.4
Morocco	4.6	1.8	-3.4	0.1
Tunisia	4.4	3.2	-3.0	-3.0

Source: International Monetary Fund.

members and supporters that exemplified a system of corruption known as 'crony capitalism'. The Moroccan economy also was performing relatively well, with GDP growth averaging over 4.6% (though economic conditions deteriorated somewhat following the 2008 European financial crisis). Given that the EU is Morocco's largest trading partner, the impact of the financial crisis led to lower revenues from tourism and workers' remittances, a rise in the budget deficit and an increase in the official unemployment rate. Although Morocco was largely spared from the 2011 unrest, the country faces similar economic problems as the rest of North Africa, including rising youth unemployment, which stood at 30% in 2011 and accounted for 44% of the working-age population.

Prior to the 2011 uprisings, the economic performance of the North African oil exporters remained positive, driven primarily by the hydrocarbons sector. State-owned enterprises, which control the majority of oil and gas production, reaped the benefits of high global oil prices, enabling them to build up international foreign reserves. Libya's National Oil Corporation (NOC), for example, produces close to 70% of the country's oil output.[3] Prior to the blockades of port facilities and labour strikes, Libyan oil exports represented 65% of GDP, 96% of export revenues, and 98% of government revenues.[4] Algeria's national oil and gas company, Sonatrach, owns about 80% of all hydrocarbon production,[5] a significant share of economic activity when hydrocarbons account for 34% of GDP, 98% of export revenues and 65% of government revenues.[6] Therefore, when the uprisings began to spread across the region, governments with significant oil revenue were better positioned than their oil-importing neighbours to respond to protesters, by offering cash transfers and hand-outs as a way to 'buy peace'.[7]

Prioritising fiscal resilience

Months of protests and street demonstrations in 2011 took a toll on economic performance across the region (Table 2). As is often the case following political turmoil, the economies of North African countries collapsed on virtually all macro-economic indicators (with the exception of Morocco). The combined effect of domestic shocks, resulting from political instability, as well as external shocks from the European financial crisis, exacerbated longstanding socio-economic problems. Moreover, as the security situation deteriorated in Libya and Tunisia, many foreign investors pulled out or held back investments and the number of tourists continued to decrease. The impact of poor security conditions, therefore, led to the outflow of foreign direct investment (FDI), reduction in tourism receipts and loss of foreign-exchange reserves.

Table 2. **North Africa: Macroeconomic indicators, 2011–14 average (percentage change)**

	GDP growth				Inflation			
	2011	2012	2013	2014	2011	2012	2013	2014
Algeria	2.8	3.7	2.3	4.6	4.5	8.9	3.3	3.0
Libya	-62.1	104.5	-13.6	-22.9	15.9	6.1	2.6	2.8
Morocco	5.0	2.7	4.4	2.9	0.9	1.3	1.9	0.4
Tunisia	-1.9	3.7	2.3	2.8	3.5	5.6	6.1	5.5

	Fiscal balance				Current-account balance			
	2011	2012	2013	2014	2011	2012	2013	2014
Algeria	-1.2	-4.1	-1.9	-7.4	9.9	5.9	0.4	-3.9
Libya	-9.0	27.8	-4.0	-43.3	9.1	29.1	13.6	-25.7
Morocco	-6.7	-7.4	-5.2	-4.9	-8.0	-9.7	-7.6	-5.8
Tunisia	-3.1	-4.7	-5.9	-4.3	-7.4	-8.2	-8.3	-7.9

Source: International Monetary Fund, REO January 2015.

Following regime change in Libya and Tunisia, economic activity declined, contracting by over 60% in Libya (Table 2). The collapse of the Libyan economy was mostly due to a drop of over 70% in oil production, which went offline during the civil war. Then, after the initial post-war recovery of much of the country's production and export capacity in 2012, production declined significantly again with new blockades as the country descended into civil war. Similarly, Tunisia had a negative growth rate of nearly 2%, after reaching 3% growth the previous year.

On the other hand, Algeria and Morocco weathered the turmoil by quickly responding to street demonstrations and increasing public spending on subsidies, wages, housing and employment programmes. In Morocco, the government of King Mohammed VI survived, despite its lack of oil wealth, and economic growth reached 5% – an impressive rate in the midst of regional turmoil. The king implemented reforms to limit his powers, through constitutional revisions and legislative elections that were held in November 2011. Algerian authorities contained protests primarily by using their hydrocarbon revenues to increase public spending by 25%, invoking memories of the Black Decade (Algeria's civil war during the 1990s), and playing up the devastating possible consequences of the uprisings.[8]

In response to widespread protests, new and old regimes in North Africa sharply increased public spending in order to quell popular discontent. In Algeria, the government increased social spending in 2011 by 12% from the year before. Similarly, in 2013 Tunisia spent nearly 60% of its budget on social expenditures (mostly food and fuel subsidies) and public-sector wage increases.

So far, foreign governments and donors have helped to stabilise public finances by providing external aid to Morocco and

Tunisia. This has come primarily from the Gulf countries (in the form of central-bank deposits to boost reserves, grants, loans or pledged investments), and through international institutions, such as the IMF, which has offered short-term financing and assistance conditional on economic reforms. The Gulf Cooperation Council countries pledged US$5 billion in aid to Morocco over five years, from 2012 onwards. Qatar has provided more than US$1 billion in grants and loans to Tunisia since 2012.

In August 2012, Morocco signed a two-year Precautionary and Liquidity Line (PLL) agreement with the IMF for US$6.2bn in external financing and in July 2014 the Executive Board of the IMF approved a second two-year PLL for an additional US$5bn in financing. Morocco opted for an IMF programme despite having a track record for implementing economic policies and economic performance. The PLL allows Morocco to draw the funds if there is a strain on finances and is meant to provide insurance against exogenous shocks, such as a rise in oil prices and spillovers from the Eurozone crisis.[9] Tunisia found itself in a more vulnerable economic position following its uprising, and signed a two-year Stand-by Arrangement in June 2013 for US$1.75bn. The goal of an IMF programme is to lay the foundation for stronger and more inclusive growth and stabilise the economy in the short term, primarily by alleviating fiscal pressures (most often by reducing energy subsidies and large wage bills).[10] Furthermore, implementing an IMF programme signals to investors and donors that the country is serious about economic reforms.

Table 3. **International reserves in North Africa, 2011–14 (US$ billion)**

	2010	2011	2012	2013	2014
Algeria	162	182	191	194	187
Libya	102	112	111	108	89
Morocco	24	21	18	19	20
Tunisia	9.5	8	9	8	8

Source: International Monetary Fund, 2015.

In contrast to Morocco and Tunisia, Algeria had sufficient foreign-exchange reserves not to seek external financing, despite declining revenues as a result of lower global oil prices (see Table 3). The Central Bank of Algeria holds close to US$190bn in international reserves. In Libya, however, due to persistent fighting that has caused a substantial loss in oil revenue, the country's once plentiful reserves have continued to decline rapidly – by nearly 25% over one year, according to Libya's Audit Bureau.[11] Until the warring factions agree to a ceasefire and acknowledge that the country cannot afford such a high public payroll, including salary payments to militias, Libya's economic outlook will remain bleak.

Initial reforms and roadblocks

The governments of Algeria, Libya, Morocco and Tunisia have continued with expansionary fiscal policies in the form of subsidies and wages, spending upwards of US$45bn annually on energy subsidies alone. For decades, subsidies have been used as a mechanism to appease populations and allow for affordable living costs. This has been easier for energy-producing Algeria and Libya, while oil importers Morocco and Tunisia have had to rapidly expand their fiscal deficits. Along with a longstanding expectation of public-sector employment, these policies have shaped the social contract that characterises all North African countries, arguably perpetuating a culture of entitlement. But as national finances have been hit, following the uprisings, by recurring strikes and sit-ins, and dwindling foreign reserves, some countries have begun to adjust their fiscal positions.

Morocco has championed the elimination of energy subsidies under the auspices of an IMF programme. The country announced in 2013 that it would cut subsidies on gasoline and fuel oil, followed by diesel; in February 2014 prices were adjusted. The cost of the subsidy system in Morocco peaked in 2012, reaching 6.6% of GDP, and in 2013 the country spent US$5bn on energy subsidies alone.[12] In Tunisia, energy subsidies account for 10% of the national budget and amount to US$2bn a year. Therefore, reducing subsidies is crucial to improving the country's fiscal position. However, it is clearly a politically sensitive issue, evidenced by the 270% increase in subsidies between 2010 and 2013. Despite push-back from influential labour unions and the middle class, the transitional government of Prime Minister Mehdi Jomaa announced in July 2014 a 6.3% hike in petroleum prices and plans for further reductions in the price of bread, sugar and other staples. Such measures aim to trim the ballooning budget deficit – estimated to reach 8% of GDP in 2014.[13]

Public-sector wages represent another area where spending needs to be cut to rein in public finances. To date, governments continue to hire public-sector workers as a measure to address high unemployment rates. In Tunisia, the public-wage bill increased by over 40% from 2010 to 2013.[14] In 2014, the government instituted a wage freeze (estimated by the IMF to save 0.4% of GDP), but continues to pay for benefits and salaries of recent hires. Similarly, Algeria's bill for public-sector wages increased by nearly 140% between 2009 and 2012. Libya, whose public sector employed roughly 85% of the labour force, increased public wages in 2011 by 30%, then again by 27% in 2012 and 20% in 2013.[15] According to IMF estimates, Morocco's wage bill remains the highest in the region, accounting for 13% of GDP in 2013.[16]

Addressing economic grievances

North African countries need a new economic model that will foster growth, promote innovation and entrepreneurship, and create jobs. This model needs to be transparent and endorsed by key stakeholders. Despite the calls for change, however, many of the Maghreb countries continue to operate central-ised or tightly regulated economic systems, which exacerbate the marginalisation of various social groups. Elites continue to oppose a more market-oriented approach, fearing they will lose out in the process. After all, this would entail transferring wealth and resources from segments of the population who have mostly benefitted from the old economic model.

As Geoff D. Porter illustrates in Chapter Four, Algeria repre-sents the most extreme version of this challenge. *Le pouvoir* – a group of unelected individuals who make key political deci-sions in Algeria – have largely gained from close, and often familial, ties to the ruling elite. It will prove extremely difficult for them to accept reforms that privatise state-owned monopo-lies and promote private-sector growth. Even in Tunisia, the new government headed by former members of Ben Ali's regime will be reluctant to undertake reforms that jeopardise their own interests or challenge the trade unions. Tunisia's interim president Moncef Marzouki recognised the need to address rising poverty rates and unemployment, but few in the country's political class have articulated a vision of what a new model of development would entail.[17]

Job creation

One of the primary causes of the Arab uprisings was the lack of economic opportunities, exemplified by the iconic image of Mohamed Bouazizi, the Tunisian fruit seller who sparked off the call for action across the region. For years, North African economies failed to produce sufficient jobs for a growing labour force constrained by structural and institutional obstacles. The problem has been compounded by rapid population growth. With a population of over 355 million, unemployment in the MENA region is among the highest in the world, hovering around 25% in the Middle East and 15% in North Africa (Table 4). This phenomenon is primarily driven by youth unemployment (for 15–24 year olds), which averages 30% – and even higher in periphery towns.[18] The IMF estimates that approximately 10.7 million people will join MENA's labour force in the coming decade, forcing regional governments to tackle unemployment in innovative ways.[19] Projected growth rates in the region are approximately half what would be required to absorb new entrants in the labour market.[20] But even when economic growth hovered around 6% a year, governments in the region proved unable to achieve job creation in any effective way.

Job creation requires a myriad of reforms, such as modifying investment regulations and updating labour-market laws, as well as identifying country-specific constraints in meeting rising demand.[21] The old strategies of expanding the public sector led to persistently high unemployment rates, low productivity, stagnant wages and growing budget deficits. In a country such as Tunisia, where sources of public revenue are limited, this is simply unsustainable.

Nevertheless, to appease protesters, regional governments have mostly dealt with unemployment by continuing to increase public-sector employment and wages, and launching employment schemes, with limited impact. Unfortunately, unemployment has not improved, as double-digit rates across the region make evident (see Table 3). Moreover, since official unemployment data do not account for those who are no longer actively seeking employment, it is difficult to accurately capture the spillover effect of unemployment into informal labour markets. These markets have developed across the region, largely because of restrictive policies that impede growth, particularly in the private sector, including excessive regulation, lack of available capital and near-monopolies in

Table 4. **Unemployment in North Africa, 2011–14 (per cent)**

	2011	2012	2013	2014
Algeria	10	10	10	11
Libya	21	20	15	30
Morocco	9	10	10	10
Tunisia	19	18	17	16

Source: World Bank MENA Economic Monitor, April 2015.

certain industries. The limited new jobs that are available are usually in the public sector, forcing young people who do not have connections to seek informal employment.

In Libya, for example, the public sector employs over 80% of the formal workforce, while the private sector employs a mere 4%.[22] Compounding the problem is a lack of budget transparency and the inability to identify employees on the government payroll. Many public employees either do not exist (known as 'shadow workers' or 'ghost workers') or collect a government paycheck without actually showing up to work, even as they earn incomes in the informal sector.

The IMF and other international financial institutions have tried to estimate the size of informal markets; in 2011 Morocco's informal economy was believed to constitute over 40% of GDP. Given that governments cannot afford to hire workers indefinitely, they must find new ways to reduce unemployment. The fastest way to create jobs in the short run is to invest in infrastructure projects. The IMF assessed that spending 1% of GDP on targeted infrastructure projects could generate as many as 18,000 jobs in Tunisia.[23] North African governments should also focus on streamlining business and investment regulations, easing barriers to market entry, promoting competition, reforming taxes and adapting labour regulations.

In the long term, reducing unemployment will require education reform and altering graduates' incentives by: offering viable alternatives to government employment; rewarding the development of technical skills; and fostering

Table 5. **Maghreb competitiveness rankings**

Report	Country Rank			
	Algeria	Libya	Morocco	Tunisia
World Bank's 2015 *Doing Business Report* (out of 189 economies)	154	188	71	60
World Economic Forum's *Global Competitiveness Report* (out of 144 economies)	79	126	72	87
Heritage Foundation's *Index of Economic Freedom* (out of 178 economies)	157	--	89	107

a culture of innovation and entrepreneurship. Other options include targeting areas outside of capital cities, where unemployment rates are higher, and providing more vocational training. Instead of increasing wages and continuously hiring workers, governments can, for example, offer one-time cash transfers to the unemployed to enrol in (re-) training programmes. Private-sector firms can also help. Pre-2011, governments tried to expand employment opportunities in the private sector, but that only benefitted those close to the regime, with no employment dividends for the majority of the population.

Moreover, private-sector growth has been frequently hampered by: stringent business regulations; restrictions to accessing credit; high taxes; and cumbersome and lengthy procedures to start a new business, register property and obtain permits (see Table 5).[24] With limited opportunities available in the private sphere, local populations have continued to turn to the public sector for employment, even after higher education. The perceived guarantee of a government job regardless of merit has altered educational preferences, leading to a mismatch between attained skills and those required to work in private companies. The ineffective allocation of human capital has also contributed to low productivity rates across North African economies, which regional governments have yet to tackle.[25]

Inclusive growth

The second socio-economic issue that led Arab citizens to the streets was steady and rising income and wealth inequalities, or lack of inclusive growth. The World Bank and OECD define inclusive growth as the pace and pattern of growth that countries undertake to ensure sustained poverty reduction. To ensure long-term growth, the participation of local populations in labour markets and the development of a multi-sectoral economy are key.[26]

Inclusive growth requires governments to undertake income-distribution schemes, by increasing taxes and tariffs, while lifting or removing politically popular subsidies. Given the looming fear of popular backlash, most North African leaders and transitional governments have delayed instituting such austerity measures as a way to salvage public finances. Those governments that have begun to cut subsidies have done so as part of an IMF programme to obtain external financing and boost investors' confidence without hydrocarbon wealth. To get their economies growing again, Tunisia and Morocco have subscribed to such programmes.

Private sector

As already discussed, governments cannot remain the employer of last resort and at the same time generate the growth necessary to absorb new entrants into the labour force. The private sector must be engaged. Given that the pro-business model has been largely discredited by local populations – who see it as a direct link to growing inequality – governments will need to foster domestic support for reforms that promote private-sector growth, such as privatisation, trade liberalisation and anti-monopoly legislation. International donors and trade partners also have a role to play. They can incentivise the region's policymakers to reform by, for example, offering trade agreements, and defining clear benchmarks to reward progress.

To 'un-crowd' private-sector development, attract investment (both domestic and foreign) and facilitate trade, governments need to adopt comprehensive and transparent regulatory frameworks while reforming existing ones. This will mean reducing trade barriers, deregulating labour laws, restructuring business and investment regulations, and reforming weak financial and legal systems. According to the World Bank's 2015 *Doing Business Report*, business regulations, excessive red tape, corruption and a poor investment climate serve as barriers to growth in North Africa. This is especially true in Algeria and Libya, which rank 154th and 188th out of 189 countries, respectively (see Table 5). Removing these barriers to growth can help unlock the region's investment potential, specifically across the tourism, agriculture and information and communications technology sectors.

Although the financial reforms recommended by international financial institutions are well known to policymakers, political decisions often trump economic policies. However, governments should leverage private-sector investment and expertise to build public-private partnerships (PPPs). These partnerships can help create jobs and improve access to social services. In Libya, for example, there are many opportunities for the government to engage the private sector in rebuilding and updating the country's outdated and crumbling infrastructure – once there is a degree of stability and a stable government.

Looking ahead

Given the current state of political transitions and economic uncertainty, governments have focused on short-term stabilisation of public finances. But policymakers urgently need to develop well-articulated economic plans that address the demands of local populations. Specifically, governments should:

1. *Prioritise short-term over long-term development goals.* There are essential macroeconomic reforms that need to be undertaken in the short term to reverse negative growth trends. These include: reforming the subsidies system; reducing the cost of starting up businesses; streamlining business regulations; reforming the tax system; developing financial sectors, advancing privatisation; promoting PPPs and downsizing government employment. Therefore, governments should prioritise which economic reforms they are willing and able to undertake in the immediate short term and devise a gradual adjustment period to ease economic burdens.

2. *Improve transparency, communication and sequencing.* Prior to undertaking reforms, governments should clearly communicate to their constituents the changes that will be forthcoming and roll out campaigns to highlight the benefits of reforms and explain protective measures. This is especially true for subsidies and shifting funds to cash transfers that target the poor. Subsidies weigh heavily on public finances; countries that have low reserves and rising fiscal deficits will be forced to reform subsidies sooner or later. Even countries flush with cash cannot sustain extensive subsidy systems, especially because their revenues depend on world oil prices. Most of the opposition to subsidy reform will come from middle-class citizens who benefit the most from lower prices. Thus, transparency and credibility are crucial to explaining where the money will be redirected, because few people trust that governments will in fact reallocate funds to protect citizens. Although subsidy reforms are important, they are only one step towards freeing

up fiscal space and easing macroeconomic constraints. Prioritising and sequencing reforms will prove crucial for elected governments operating in a highly politicised environment with high expectations.

3. *Work with international actors to provide economic incentives for change.* The   international community can play a major role in offering Libya, Morocco and Tunisia incentives to move towards a free-market economy. It will be harder in the case of Algeria because of the country's closed political system, but not impossible if neighbouring countries benefit from closer economic ties with trading partners. The European Union (EU) has already taken steps towards offering North African countries greater access to European markets, but more can be done. Morocco, for example, is negotiating a framework for a comprehensive and deep free-trade area agreement with the EU. If successful, this model can be transferred to other North African countries and would incentivise them to undertake market reforms to ensure European partnerships. Similarly, the United States (US) can relaunch negotiations of the 2002 Trade and Investment Framework Agreement to complement ongoing technical and economic assistance for private-sector development. A free-trade agreement with the US will provide the Tunisian authorities with a framework for economic development and reforms. Similarly, in 2012 the US government established the Tunisian-American Enterprise Fund, well capitalised at US$60 million, to invest in economic growth and job creation in Tunisia.

Notes

1   For example, in Tunisia, Articles 10 and 16 of the investment code stipulate that firms that export at least 70% of their output do not have to pay profit and turnover taxes. According to a World Bank study, 'All in the Family: State Capture in Tunisia', 'this has helped Tunisia attract foreign investors and accolades from the international community, despite the onshore sector being highly protected and largely closed to foreign competition.' See Bob Rijkers, Caroline Freundand and Antonio Nucifora, 'All in the Family: State Capture in Tunisia', Policy Research Working Paper, no. 6810, March 2014, http://documents.worldbank.org/curated/en/2014/03/19291754/all-family-state-capture-tunisia.

2   US Energy Information Administration, 'Libya: Country Report', October 2013, http://www.eia.gov/countries/cab.cfm?fps=ly.

3   Ibid.

4   Mohsin Khan and Karim Mezran, 'The Libyan Economy After the Revolution: Still No Clear Vision', Atlantic Council, 28 August 2013, http://www.atlanticcouncil.org/publications/issue-briefs/the-libyan-economy-after-the-revolution-still-no-clear-vision.

5   'Algeria: Country Report', US Energy Information Administration, May 2013, http://www.eia.gov/countries/analysisbriefs/Algeria/algeria.pdf.

6   Mohsin Khan and Karim Mezran, 'No Arab Spring for Algeria', Atlantic Council, May 2014, http://www.atlanticcouncil.org/images/publications/No_Arab_Spring_for_Algeria.pdf.

7   Mohsin Khan and Svetlana Milbert, 'Middle East Protests: Can Money Buy Peace?', Peterson Institute Real Time Economic Issues Watch, 9 March 2011, http://blogs.piie.com/realtime/?p=2068.

8   Khan and Mezran, 'No Arab Spring for Algeria'; 'Algeria: 2013 Article IV Consultation', IMF Country Report, no. 14/32, February 2014.

9   'Morocco Taps $6.2 Billion Precautionary Loan from IMF', IMF Survey Magazine, 3 August 2012, http://www.imf.org/external/pubs/ft/survey/so/2012/car080312b.htm.

10 'Tunisia: Request for a Stand-By Arrangement—Staff Report', IMF Country Report, no. 13/161, June 2013.

11 From end-2013 to end-2014. See Feras Bosalum and Ulf Laessing, 'Libya's Foreign Reserves Fell by a Quarter Last Year,' Reuters, 4 May 2015, http://af.reuters.com/article/commoditiesNews/idAFL5N0XV2SI20150504?pageNumber=1&virtualBrandChannel=0.

12 Paolo Verme, Khalid El-Massnaoui and Abdelkrim Araar, 'Reforming Subsidies in Morocco', Economic Premise, no. 134, February 2014.

13 Tarek Amara, 'Tunisia Raises Petrol Prices by 6.3 Percent to Trim Budget Gap', Reuters, 1 July 2014, http://uk.reuters.com/article/2014/07/01/tunisia-energy-idUKL6N0PC3OI20140701.

14 'Tunisia: Third Review Under the Stand-By Arrangement,

Request for Modification of Performance Criteria and Waiver of Applicability', *IMF Country Report*, no. 14/123, May 2014.

[15] Khan and Mezran, 'The Libyan Economy After the Revolution'.

[16] 'Morocco: 2013 Article IV Consultation', *IMF Country Report*, no. 14/65, March 2014.

[17] 'Tunisia Needs a New Economic Model to End Poverty', Morocco World News, 30 March 2013, http://www.moroccoworldnews. com/2013/03/84674/tunisia-needs- new-economic-model-to-end- poverty-president-2/.

[18] 'The Arab World Competitiveness Report', World Economic Forum, 6 March 2013, http://www3. weforum.org/docs/WEF_AWCR_ Report_2013.pdf.

[19] Masood Ahmed, 'Youth Unemployment in the MENA Region: Determinants and Challenges', World Economic Forum, June 2012.

[20] United Nations Development Programme and International Labour Organization, 'Rethinking Economic Growth: Towards Productive and Inclusive Arab Societies', 2012, http://www.ilo. org/wcmsp5/groups/public/--- arabstates/---ro-beirut/documents/ publication/wcms_208346.pdf.

[21] Gita Subrahmanyam et al., 'Tackling Youth Unemployment in the Maghreb', African Development Bank Economic Brief, 2011, http://www.unevoc.unesco.org/ fileadmin/up/subrahmanyam_-_ tackling_youth_unemployment_ in_the_maghreb.pdf.

[22] 'Growth Slowdown Heightens the Need for Reforms', *MENA Quarterly Economic Brief*, no. 2, January 2014.

[23] Masood Ahmed, 'Creating Jobs in the Middle East and North Africa', *Asharq Al Awsat*, 20 May 2011, https://www.imf.org/external/np/ vc/2011/052011.htm.

[24] 'Doing Business 2014: Understanding Regulations for Small and Medium-Size Enterprises', *Doing Business*, no. 11, 29 October 2013.

[25] Roberta Gatti et al., *Jobs for Shared Prosperity: Time for Action in the Middle East and North Africa* (Washington DC: World Bank, 22 April 2013).

[26] Elena Ianchovichina, Susanna Lundstrom and Leonardo Garrido, 'What is Inclusive Growth?', World Bank, 10 February 2009, http://siteresources. worldbank.org/INTDEBTDEPT/ Resources/468980-1218567884549/ WhatIsInclusiveGrowth20081230. pdf.

CONCLUSION

The Challenges on Implementing Institutional Reform

Ben Fishman

As the previous pages detail, there was a wide variation in how states and societies in North Africa responded to the Arab uprisings of 2011. While this book is only a first attempt at analysing what happened in the region, several conclusions can be drawn already. Firstly, North Africa requires a sustained and wholesale emphasis on reforming institutions and improving the quality of governance – in security, economics, and public services – if it is ever to fulfil the initial optimism of 2011. Security without economic growth may improve short-term stability but will not address popular demands for opportunity and dignity. Conversely, without security, government and citizen initiatives will be vulnerable to the ever-growing threats of jihadist terrorism or extrajudicial violence – especially in Libya. Of course, states cannot make equal progress on all fronts at once. The approaches of governments must be tailored to their specific needs and priorities. For example, the strong security apparatus in Algeria could facilitate a period of more intensive political and economic reforms, if the elite can be convinced of their need. In Libya, on the other hand, a baseline of security must be established to end the civil war, followed by a massive overhaul of the Gadhafi-era government, before the political reforms envisioned in 2011 can be realised.

Secondly, institution-building efforts should include intra-regional cooperation within North Africa where virtually none exists today. Actors from the broader Middle East have proved all too eager to exploit this lack of cooperation to advance their own interests in Morocco, Algeria, Libya and Tunisia. The problem is that the United States (US) and European Union (EU) are less invested in developments in North Africa than Egypt, Turkey and the wealthy Gulf states, which are willing to devote more resources with fewer conditions.[1] Given this asymmetry, the most effective way for the West to maintain its influence is by targeting its assistance on institution-building programmes in the fields of security, governance and finance where it can offer the most professionalism and expertise – for example: improving police forces and training the judicial sector; promoting adoption of public-sector reforms to fight corruption and improve transparency; and revising tax codes and collection methods.

Finally, there are lessons from North Africa's experiences that could be applied to the broader Middle East in the aftermath of the uprisings.

Institutional reform

The most striking differences in the responses of the four North African states to the Arab uprisings of 2011 lie in the nature and structure of their respective regime institutions.

In the case of Tunisia, Zine al-Abidine Ben Ali's departure obviously created difficulties but did not lead to a complete collapse of the state, in part because some key institutions and technocrats remained. The manner in which Ben Ali fled the country relatively quickly allowed the regime to avoid being held fully responsible for his and his family's misdeeds.

Ben Ali and his inner circle lost their legitimacy almost overnight, the last-ditch promises to reform rang empty, and the police state he had built cracked, unwilling or unable to inflict mass casualties on the population.

After some initial turmoil, the first interim government was led by a former veteran politician, Caid Essebsi, who assumed the role of interim prime minister. Essebsi gave up power once the National Constituent Assembly elections were held. The military – relatively small but symbolic – remained neutral throughout the revolutionary and post-revolutionary periods, making clear that its sole function was to protect the people. The influential trade unions preserved their status, contributing to the relative stability, and eventually played a timely political role by mediating the constitutional stand-off between the leadership of the Islamist Ennahda and secular Nidaa Tounes parties. Finally, Tunisians turned to the independence-era constitution as a basis to establish a new legal framework for the country.

This was in sharp contrast to the circumstances in Libya where the state virtually disintegrated after Gadhafi's demise. Over the years, Gadhafi had built Libya for himself and his immediate family, while using the country's oil wealth to fund extensive subsidies and government jobs to placate the population as needed. He had constructed the ultimate Kafkaesque bureaucracy; decisions were perpetually deferred to contradictory organisations, which only Gadhafi or his family members could resolve. Salaries were paid to hundreds of thousands of state employees who rarely showed up to work if their jobs existed at all. Units of the military that protected the regime received funding and training, while the rest of the armed forces were neglected out of fear of a potential coup. It was no wonder that virtually no viable security apparatus could be resurrected by the transitional authorities after the revolution.

A deadly post-revolutionary conflict emerged between Islamist militias that wanted to continue the revolution against all elements of the old regime, including those military officers who had defected and fought against Gadhafi's forces in 2011, and officers who sought a role in the post-revolutionary state. As Borzou Daragahi documents in Chapter Two, Islamist militias pitted against secular/liberal groups represent just one rivalry in the multi-dimensional civil war that plagues Libya today.[2]

When the National Transitional Council (NTC) took power following Gadhafi's death and subsequently appointed an interim government to manage state affairs, it proved unable to reform Gadhafi's system of government, partly because a series of former exiles serving in top posts did not fully appreciate the extent of Libya's problems. Small-scale international efforts to help build capacity in ministries were unable to make meaningful progress, especially amid deepening security challenges. Ministers lacked budget authority over their ministries, in part because the NTC and later the General National Congress (GNC) refused to streamline laws left over from the Gadhafi era that restricted ministerial authorities. And despite endless offers of assistance to the interim authorities, the international community could hardly gain traction because Libyans simply did not know how to sign appropriate documents and follow through on their commitments.[3] In hindsight, no one wanted to take responsibility for decisions and be blamed if something went wrong – another burden of the Gadhafi era.

These phenomena contributed significantly to the subsequent political paralysis and militia violence that Daragahi describes. No interim body was capable of filling the vacuum left by Gadhafi's demise. Despite the successful election in July 2012 of Libya's first democratically elected legislature, the failure to improve governance in 2012 and 2013 led to the chaos that envelops the country today, with two governments and multiple militia movements vying for authority and the United Nations struggling to forge a government of national accord and a ceasefire that will stick.

Another factor has contributed to Libya's instability. Historically, Libya has been a country consisting of three distinct regions: Tripolitania in the west, Cyrenaica in the east and Fezzan in the south. These regional divisions have split the country on multiple fronts since 2011 and demonstrated how Libyans have struggled to unite behind a single concrete issue since Gadhafi's overthrow. They also created significant tension when crafting the initial electoral framework for the GNC, as the various parties sought to ensure their communities would be appropriately represented. An on-again, off-again series of oil boycotts also began as factions vied for equitable distribution of oil revenue across the country. Finally, the country was split between two rival governments for much of 2014 and 2015, as each constructed narratives of legitimacy while ignoring the raging civil war. All this underscores the enormous challenges ahead for a country of multiple clashing identities: west vs. east; urban vs. tribal; old regime members vs. revolutionaries; Islamist vs. non-Islamist; Berber vs. Arab; returning expatriates vs. Gadhafi-era politicians. In many ways, the 2012 elections pushed these serious tensions under the table. But, at some point, Libyans will have to address these questions if the country is going to survive in its present form.

The importance of institutions is further evidenced by the ability of Morocco and Algeria to effectively respond to public pressure for change. Although Algeria was able to direct its hydrocarbon wealth to increased government spending that addressed protesters' concerns, the leadership would have undoubtedly been more vulnerable were it not for the relative unity of *le pouvoir*. Had there been divisions within the elite at the time – and extending into the period of Bouteflika's 2014 re-election campaign – popular demands for reform would almost certainly have increased. Instead, *le pouvoir* kept most of their feuds away from public view and recognised, as Geoff Porter describes in Chapter Four, the overall imperative to preserve the system. Algeria's most significant institution thus survived, and with it, the loyalty of the military and Sonatrach, the state-led oil and gas company that enabled the increase in public spending. Nevertheless, *le pouvoir* has its weaknesses, as Porter details, and will face a crucial test with the eventual successor of President Bouteflika. The Algerian state must continue to reform and modernise its economy, in particular, if it wishes to avoid future political threats.

Similarly, Morocco's relative success in responding to the upheaval of 2011 can be attributed to the institution of the monarchy and its ability to act decisively when pressed hard enough. By announcing constitutional reforms and free elections in March 2011, King Mohammed VI took advantage of his position of power to enact meaningful changes – or what were at least viewed as meaningful by a public mostly willing to give him a chance. Only extremists questioned the monarchy's legitimacy. Moreover, the king distanced himself from the newly elected government, enabling the palace to blame the country's economic problems on the Islamist prime minister and his team. This situation may not be sustainable, but as Haim Malka highlights in Chapter Three, it demonstrates the king's ability to act when circumstances demand a response, taking advantage of his resources, including foreign support, as well as the inherent legitimacy he derives as a monarch and descendant of the Prophet.

Why institutions matter

At a time when the George W. Bush administration was pursuing democracy in Iraq and pressing for broader reforms across the Middle East, political scientists Jack Snyder and Edward Mansfield cautioned that democracy promotion was frequently destabilising unless prior efforts were made in institution-building. As Snyder and Mansfield note: 'It is better to strengthen state institutions that can serve as the basis for an inclusive, civic form of national loyalty before spurring popular political action that could, in their absence, play into the hands of exclusionary ethnic national movements.'[4] In other words, elections without agreement on the contours of a state and the requirements of its institutions may provoke identity-driven politics (defined by tribal, geographic or religious loyalties in the case of North Africa) and endanger the very process of democratic transition. Issues around religious identity, political representation or control of a country's natural resources can easily derail transition if they are not at least partly resolved during or immediately after the revolutionary moment. Nowhere has this proven truer than in Libya.

Undoubtedly, building institutions in advance of an electoral democracy may be unrealistic when a population is demanding change or, in more extreme cases, the overthrow of the regime. It also raises several questions, including how much institution-building is required before a state is 'ready' for democracy. But Snyder and Mansfield generally are correct that democratisation will be worse off in states with weaker institutions.

Similarly, Francis Fukuyama observes that sustainable institution-building requires a home-grown demand for change – precisely what the Arab uprisings represented in North Africa in 2011 (as opposed to change imposed by force). As Fukuyama notes, 'what is most urgent for the majority of developing countries is to increase the basic strength of their state institutions to supply those core functions that only governments can provide.'[5] This suggests that in post-2011 North Africa, the next stage of political development for each country should involve a concerted effort to improve institutional capacities and the state's ability to deliver services, carry out economic reforms and provide security, while respecting basic rights of citizens. Otherwise, Morocco and Algeria could face renewed and higher-intensity protests, Tunisia's democratic transition could begin to backslide if the economy continues to stagnate, and Libya will only continue its self-destruction.

Economics and security

The key issues of the Arab uprisings – the search for dignity and opportunity – were about economics as much as politics. However, on the economic front, as Svetlana Milbert details in Chapter Six, North African states are just beginning to scratch the surface of necessary reforms. These will require cultural shifts in addition to changes of policy.

The temptation to conduct business as usual remains high, particularly for vulnerable governments seeking to establish their legitimacy. Few political parties are willing to campaign on the need to cut subsidies and government jobs when that is what is ultimately required to reduce budget deficits and enable greater investments in education, vocational training and social-welfare spending. Governments and emerging political parties must do a better job in articulating these priorities to their constituents if they are going to garner public support for such policies. Actions that would pay immediate dividends for North African economies would be to focus on easing regulations and bureaucratic inefficiencies, and to crack down on corruption that stymies private-sector growth and entrepreneurial endeavours.[6] In its ease of doing business report in 2014, the World Bank ranked Tunisia 60th, Morocco 71st, Algeria 154th and Libya 188th. However, when considering rankings for starting a business and getting credit, Tunisia ranks 100th and 116th respectively and Morocco ranks 54th and 104th respectively. In practical terms, it takes an average of 85 days to obtain a construction permit and 20 days to import goods in Tunisia.[7] If job creation is to become a priority, these global rankings have to shift considerably.[8] As Milbert outlines, the IMF is actively assisting these countries with developing reforms, but it will require local political leaders to communicate the need for reforms to their supporters if they want to avoid popular uprisings in the future. Suspicions of public corruption will also remain in these countries unless governments adopt greater transparency measures, with the active participation of non-governmental organisations.

On the security front, North Africa faces jihadist threats both due to its history of violent extremism and the potential return of fighters from Iraq and Syria, especially those seeking to exploit the anarchy in Libya. This will only worsen as the country's politics remain deadlocked and an accepted government fails to materialise. As Jean-Pierre Filiu details, the jihadist challenge to North Africa is complex and ever-evolving. The dangers posed by North African jihadists fighting with the Islamic State of Iraq and al-Sham (ISIS) will certainly exacerbate regional security in the long term. According to 2014 estimates, Tunisians constitute the largest number of fighters – 3,000 in total – who have travelled to Syria or Iraq (although not all have joined ISIS). An estimated 1,500 Moroccans are now fighting with the organisation, as well as more than 500 Libyans.[9] The US-led coalition to counter ISIS, must, therefore, work closely with its North African partners to develop strategies that deter foreign fighters from leaving to fight and better handle their return. Such strategies could involve closer monitoring, de-radicalisation programmes and imprisonment of the worst offenders. So far, though, the jihadist problem facing North Africa has not received nearly enough attention from the coalition. For example, despite multiple trips to the Middle East, Europe and Asia, Gen. John Allen, the special US presidential envoy for the global coalition to counter ISIS, has yet to travel to North Africa.[10]

A key challenge in improving state security institutions in North Africa will be achieving the necessary balance between respecting individual rights and disrupting jihadist and criminal networks effectively. Every country is in need of significant security-sector reform – a combination of investigative, judicial and penal measures that can ultimately build a society based on the rule of law rather than the practice of arbitrary arrests, torture and detentions. In fact, an argument can be made that the uprisings of 2011, especially against Gadhafi, were as much a rebellion against cruel systems of oppression as about demands for economic dignity. Moreover, tactics employed by heavy-handed security institutions have exacerbated the problem of home-grown jihadism at least as much as they have caught terrorists. The example of Moncef Marzouki – the interim president of Tunisia and former prisoner of conscience – is rare; more common is the example of Abou Iyad, the Salafist extremist implicated in the 2012 attack on the US Embassy in Tunis, who was released as part of a general amnesty during Tunisia's revolution and is now in hiding.

Reforming security institutions will require a great commitment by leaders and cooperation among their traditional bases of power. As Malka and Porter note, in Algeria and Morocco – two of the most stable regimes in the region – unrest could be sparked off by an excessive abuse of power in the security sphere, such as a high-profile case of torture or imprisonment. Finding the right balance between security-sector reform and tackling the growing threat of extremism will, therefore, remain a vexing challenge for North Africa and the broader Middle East.

Lack of regional cooperation

What also stands out from the preceding pages is the absence of meaningful cooperation among North African states in either security or economic affairs. According to the World Bank, intra-regional trade represented less than 2% of North Africa's combined GDP and less than 3% of its total trade in 2007. A 2006 World Bank study suggested that per-capita GDP growth in Algeria, Morocco and Tunisia could double between 2005 and 2015 with serious steps toward integration, such as reducing trade barriers and promoting financial integration. Unfortunately, such efforts have not transpired. The IMF began advising North African countries on trade facilitation, financial integration, promotion of the private sector and joint projects in 2005, and finance ministers and central bank governors have met regularly, but to little avail. Christine Lagarde, the IMF's director-general, sounded a somewhat more optimistic note when she joined the fifth meeting of regional finance ministers and central bank governors in January 2013 and cited, in particular, an agreement to establish the Maghreb Bank for Investment and Foreign Trade (MBICE) – a regional bank to encourage private-sector development.

As with the adoption of country-specific economic reforms, regional economic integration will require as much of a change in culture as it will in policy. Certainly, little progress can be expected as long as poor relations persist between Morocco and Algeria, and Libya remains unstable. Despite several attempts at mending Algeria–Morocco relations, including a UN-mediation effort over the disputed Western Sahara, neither country appears any closer to improving ties, leaving their border shut for the past 20 years. Opening the border would certainly increase trade, reduce smuggling and create job opportunities. Of course, changing the status quo would require taking on influential groups; elites on both sides of the border have profited from the high prices with the current set-up.[11]

In the foreseeable future, trade with Europe and partnerships with international financial institutions may provide the most likely incentive structure to encourage much-needed economic reforms in the individual countries of North Africa, as Milbert argues, but the idea of intra-regional trade and economic unions should not be forgotten. At a minimum, the IMF and World Bank should facilitate regular meetings of regional economic officials, and if constructive ideas emerge they should be presented to North African governments.

Similarly, on the security front, North Africa would benefit significantly from more institutionalised cooperation; countries currently rely on ad hoc arrangements and occasional encounters between security chiefs. Algeria and Tunisia have the most effective regional cooperation against al-Qaeda in the Islamic Maghreb and its offshoots in the Jebel ech Chambi mountains in western Tunisia, which abut Algeria's northern border. The area is beset by militants who have launched a number of attacks against Tunisia's poorly equipped military, though Algeria has been a helpful ally in this fight.

The situation in Libya is far more complicated because of the absence of an effective government to combat cross-border threats, even if it had the will to do so. Although Algeria closed its border with Libya in May 2014, Tunisia did not, mainly because of the economic benefits created by the stream of Libyans taking advantage of Tunisian healthcare and other goods.[12] That changed once Tunisia believed that the perpetrators of terrorist attacks in March and June had trained in Libya. Both Algeria and Tunisia have threatened to build fences along their borders with Libya – a massive endeavour that would only mildly deter or reroute determined smugglers and militants.

Effective security cooperation in North Africa will be difficult until Libya stabilises and a civilian government takes control of a nascent military that requires significant training. But that does not mean that a framework for greater security cooperation should not be developed now, particularly because it will take some time to overcome long-standing suspicions about international intervention in the region's affairs – particularly in Algeria.

Positive steps have been made towards greater intra-regional security cooperation. The General Staff Joint-Operations Committee (CEMOC) was created in 2010 by Algeria, Niger, Mauritania and Mali to increase collaboration against AQIM and other extremist groups.[13] So far, the organisation, based in southern Algeria, does not fully operate like a joint command but has the potential to increase capacity and include the participation of other states beyond the region, such as France and the US. The French-led *Operation Serval*, discussed in Chapter Five, in which Algeria opened its airspace to France and allied planes, may provide a precedent for such international security cooperation.

Ultimately, North Africa should aim to pursue an arrangement similar to the Gulf Cooperation Council (GCC), which, over the past decade, and with US assistance, has built up significant defence capabilities. These include modernised military hardware, ballistic-missile defence and critical infrastructure protection, which were considered impossible just a few years ago due to similar rivalries that plague North Africa today.

The lack of intra-regional cooperation has left room for outside interference by those who have a stake in the post-revolutionary politics of North Africa. The most direct case has been Libya, where opposing sides in the civil war have been supported by pro- and anti-Islamist countries, dating back to the 2011 revolution. At first, Qatar was the most prominent supporter of the Islamist militias in eastern Libya, as well as the coalition of militias in Misrata. The UAE, on the other hand, supported revolutionary brigades out of the Nafusa Mountains. This changed once the civil war between the Dignity (anti-Islamist) and Dawn (Islamist and Misratan) coalitions heated up as an extension of the UAE and Egypt's regional campaign against Islamists of all stripes. Starting in the spring of 2014, these countries began backing Gen. Haftar's bombings. While Qatar has limited its overt support of the Dawn coalition due to concerns about maintaining GCC unity, Turkey has defended the Islamist coalitions, potentially also supplying arms.[14]

Although these regional actors pay lip service to UN-led negotiations to form a unity government, their actions will only prolong the Libyan civil war and fragmentation of the state – an outcome that would benefit the jihadists. To counter this trend, the US and EU must actively promote security and development, and encourage regional actors to play a constructive role in the UN's peace plan and national-dialogue effort. For example, the West should insist that all countries, especially its allies, abide by the arms embargo that has never been truly enforced since it was first imposed by the UN in 2011. Unfortunately, with so many other questions in the Middle East looming over the US–GCC alliance – primarily the Iran nuclear deal, the struggle against ISIS and civil wars in Syria and Yemen – Libya is likely to remain a second-order issue for the foreseeable future.

Even in Tunisia and Morocco, a growing asymmetry exists between the reach of the West and that of the wider Middle East. In 2011, the GCC committed to provide Morocco with US$2.5 billion over five years. Similarly, Qatar and Turkey each provided Tunisia with loans worth US$500 million in 2012, largely to support the governing Islamist Ennahda Party. More importantly, this assistance does not come with the same kind of conditions that Western assistance involves (Milbert details typical IMF loan requirements in Chapter Six). The more financial aid the Gulf offers to North African states, the less incentive they have to make economic reforms necessary for job creation. Here too, coordination is key. By defining stability as a continuation of the status quo in North Africa – and prioritising defence against all forms of Islamism – the Gulf states and Egypt are in fact risking a prolonged period of instability. One thing is clear: Western interests will remain misaligned unless the US and EU begin a more direct dialogue with regional friends to try to find a common basis for engaging in North Africa. Crucially, the US and EU can offer help in building the governance and security institutions needed to promote job growth and safety, ideally with complementary funding from regional partners for development and infrastructure projects.

Regional lessons

The diverse experiences of North Africa over the past four years offer some lessons for the broader Middle East. Firstly, ongoing reform and good governance are necessary regardless of the degree of development or wealth of the state. With the probable exceptions of Qatar and the UAE due to their wealth and very small and homogenous populations, states in the Middle East can expect new phases of instability for as long as they fail to appreciate the lessons of 2011 and the demands of their citizens for dignity and political and economic opportunity. The old models of state-led repression have proved to be ineffective; it would be a catastrophic mistake to return to them. Perhaps Saudi Arabia and Kuwait can insulate themselves from such problems for a decade or so and follow the Algerian model of massive social spending during times of turmoil. But sooner or later, the challenges of exploding youth populations and untargeted spending will catch up with them. Planning for that inevitability should start now.

For states with limited financial resources, the Moroccan model may prove instructive, so long as the reforms remain steady and do not backslide. The closest parallel is Jordan, where King Abdullah initiated a process in 2011 that promised many of the same reforms as Morocco. The major difference, however, was that post-2011 elections produced an Islamist-led government in Morocco and a loyalist government in Jordan (the Jordanian Muslim Brotherhood boycotted the January 2013 election and the electoral system heavily favoured the historic East Bank constituency loyal to the monarchy). Regardless of the formula and pace of adopting reforms, Morocco must not only voice a clear willingness to improve governance and political access for its citizens, but also follow through on those commitments. As long as populations can point to progress on those fronts, they are more likely to accept incremental, rather than revolutionary, change.

When a leader responds to a revolutionary movement dismissively or with such brutality that he loses the support of key segments of the population and international community, is civil war followed by state failure inevitable? The lessons of post-Gadhafi Libya suggest that state-building after a revolution is extremely challenging, particularly when the former regime devoted so much time to weakening institutions and isolating the country from the rest of the world. One lesson is that the international community needs to be far more involved in the post-revolutionary stabilisation and reconstruction process, including enforcing ceasefires and protecting state institutions and critical infrastructure. Security and stability are the building blocks for any international assistance programme on governance, development or economics. The UN or similar impartial organisations can lead a national dialogue to establish agreed parameters of the state that can form the basis of a constitution and a reconciliation process. Tunisia's model of electing a constituent assembly before a legislature may prove effective in some cases, but risks getting bogged down in matters of everyday bureaucracy and budgets (as Libya's National Transitional Council did). When the Syrian civil war eventually ends, these lessons may prove valuable, but it will of course depend on how the war ends, whether the state fragments, and who is left standing after more than four years of devastation already.

Will Tunisia be all that remains of the initial optimism of 2011? The country has undergone hard-earned progress towards a democratic transition, which was almost derailed after two politically motivated assassinations in 2013, as Nicole Rowsell details in Chapter One. Nonetheless, Tunisians will have a difficult road ahead if the new parliament and government prove unable to address vexing economic and security challenges, including an increasing terrorist threat for which it has not adequately prepared.[15]

Arguably, the example of Tunisia is unique because of its small population, its relatively high GDP per capita (Tunisia is the wealthiest non-energy exporting country in the region[16]), the neutral role of the military during the revolution, and the balance of power between Islamist and secular parties who recognise that neither can have a monopoly on power. The 2015 Nobel Peace Prize, which was awarded to the four civil-society organisations that sponsored the critical national dialogue, highlights another strength of Tunisian political life. The personal appeal of Ennahda leader Rached Ghannouchi (and his insistence that Islam and democracy are compatible) and President Caid Essebsi also helped the country's democratic transition.

The broader point remains that North Africa – and the rest of the Middle East – should be evaluated not primarily in terms of democratisation, which is still a distant reality for most countries, but in terms of the commitment to implementing institutional reforms in the security, governance and economic spheres. Such an approach can help stabilise relations between states and societies, which in turn will encourage more active citizen participation in state affairs.

Notes

1   Haim Malka, 'Maghreb Rising: Competition and Realignment' in John Alterman (ed.) *Rocky Harbors: Taking Stock of Middle East in 2015,* Center for Strategic and International Studies, 3 April, 2015: http://csis.org/files/publication/150403_Malka_RockyHarbors_chapter7_0.pdf.

2   See also Frederic Wehrey, 'Ending Libya's Civil War: Reconciling Politics, Rebuilding Security', Carnegie Endowment for International Peace, 24 September 2014, http://carnegieendowment.org/2014/09/24/ending-libya-s-civil-war-reconciling-politics-rebuilding-security/hpv4.

3   Derek Chollet and Ben Fishman, 'Who Lost Libya', *Foreign Affairs,* May/June 2015, https://www.foreignaffairs.com/articles/libya/2015-04-20/who-lost-libya.

4   Edward D. Mansfield and Jack Snyder, 'Prone to Violence: The Paradox of the Democratic Peace', *National Interest,* Winter 2005/2006.

5   Francis Fukuyama, *State Building: Governance and World Order in the 21st Century* (Ithaca, NY: Cornell University Press, 2004), p. 42.

6   For example, Wamda emerged after 2011 to report on and connect aspiring entrepreneurs; http://www.wamda.com/country/tunisia.

7   Ian Talley, 'IMF Chief Urges Tunisia to Speed Up Reforms,' *Wall Street Journal,* 9 Sept., 2015: http://www.wsj.com/articles/imf-chief-urges-tunisia-to-speed-up-reforms-1441842987; World Bank, 'Doing Business: Trading Across Borders, Tunisia', http://www.doingbusiness.org/data/exploreeconomies/tunisia/trading-across-borders/.

8   World Bank, 'Doing Business: Measuring Business Regulations', http://www.doingbusiness.org/rankings.

9   'European Jihadists: Why and How Westerners Go to Fight in Syria and Iraq', *The Economist,* 30 August 2014, http://www.economist.com/news/middle-east-and-africa/21614226-why-and-how-westerners-go-fight-syria-and-iraq-it-aint-half-hot-here-mum.

10 The presidential envoy's trips are listed on the US Department of State's website: http://www.state.gov/r/pa/prs/ps/2014/index.htm.

11 Vish Sakthivel, 'Kerry's Visit to Morocco and Algeria: Navigating Between Competitors', Washington

Institute Policy Watch, 4 November 2013, http://www. washingtoninstitute.org/policy-analysis/view/kerrys-visit-to-morocco-and-algeria-navigating-between-competitors.

12 Carlotta Gall, 'Libyan Refugees Stream to Tunisia for Care and Tell of a Home That is Torn Apart', *New York Times*, 9 September 2014, http://www.nytimes.com/2014/09/10/world/africa/libya-refugees-tunisia-tripoli.html.

13 Yahia H. Zoubir and Louisa Dris-Aït-Hamadouche, *Global Security Watch – The Maghreb: Algeria, Libya, Morocco, and Tunisia* (ABC-CLIO, 2013).

14 UN Security Council, 'Final Report of the Panel of Experts Established Pursuant to Resolution 1973', 2011, http://www.security councilreport.org/atf/cf/%7B65BF CF9B-6D27-4E9C-8CD3-CF6E4 FF96FF9%7D/s_2015_128.pdf.

15 Ben Fishman, 'Tunisia Needs to do More to Fight Terrorism', *National Interest*, 13 July 2015, http://www. nationalinterest.org/feature/tunisia-needs-do-more-fight-terrorism-13315.

16 Renaissance Capital, 'The revolutionary nature of growth', 22 June 2011, http://www. fastestbillion.com/res/Research/Revolutionary_growth-220611.pdf.

INDEX

A

King Abdullah (Jordan) 146
Abou Iyad al-Tounissi 101, 102, 103, 104, 140
Abou Zeid, Abdelhamid 99, 100, 106, 107, 108, 109
Afghanistan 98, 101, 103, 109
African Union 108
Algeria 9, 11, 12, 13, 14, 15, 16, 17, 18, 71, 79–96,
    97, 98, 99, 100, 101, 105, 107, 108, 109, 110, 115,
    116, 117, 118, 119, 120, 121, 123, 124, 126, 128,
    131, 132, 135, 136, 138, 140, 141, 142, 143, 145
    Barakat movement 85
    Black Decade 117
    Black Spring 92, 93
    Boumerdes Mountains 89
    Central Bank 119
    Forum des Chefs d'Entreprise 90, 92
    In Amenas gas-plant attack 16, 80, 89, 91, 94, 109
    Islamic Armed Group 98, 99
    Le pouvoir 81, 83, 85, 121, 135, 136
    National Liberation Front 81, 91
    Salafist Group for Preaching and Combat 99, 100
    Sonatrach 115
Algiers (Algeria) 89, 93, 99
al-Haqed 73
Ali, Ahmed 55
al-Ali, Zaid 53
Allen, John 140
al-Mourabitoun 14, 94, 95, 98, 106, 109, 111
al-Qaeda 16, 48, 89, 94, 97, 101, 102, 103, 105
al-Qaeda in the Islamic Maghreb 89, 94, 95, 98,
    100, 101, 105, 106, 107, 108, 109, 110, 111, 142,
    143
Ansar al-Sharia 14, 29, 30, 45, 46, 48, 51, 54, 98,
    102, 103, 104
Ansar al-Sharia (Libya) 103
Arab League 13
Arab Maghreb Union 13

Arab uprisings 10, 12, 18, 113, 121, 131, 132, 137, 138
Arlit (Niger) 106, 109
Asia 9, 140

B

Badi, Salah 46
al-Baghdadi, Abu Bakr 41, 110, 111
Bahrain 10, 114
Baida (Libya) 47
Bamako (Mali) 107, 108, 110
Belaïd, Chokri 29, 104
Belhaj, Abdelhakim 45, 103
Belkhadem, Abdelaziz 91
Belmokhtar, Mokhtar 89, 94, 95, 98, 99, 100, 106,
    107, 108, 109
Ben Ali, Leila 22
Ben Ali, Zine al-Abidine 10, 13, 14, 15, 19, 21, 22,
    23, 24, 27, 34, 36, 101, 114, 121, 132, 133
Benflis, Ali 81
Benghazi (Libya) 40, 41, 47, 53, 103, 104
Benhassine, Seifallah 101
Benkirane, Abdelilah 63
Berbers 12
bin Laden, Osama 99, 102, 111
Bouazizi, Mohamed 22, 121
Bourguiba, Habib 20, 21
Bouteflika, Abdelaziz 13, 79, 80, 81, 82, 83, 85, 91,
    93, 94, 95, 136
BP (UK) 16
Bugaighis, Salwa 52
Burkina Faso 106
Bush, George W. 136

C

Casablanca (Morocco)
    2003 bombings 62, 63, 68
Chad 108

D
Damascus (Syria) 11
Derna (Libya) 51, 111
Drah, Mohamed Salah 40
Droukdel, Abdelmalek 99, 100, 107, 109

E
Eastern Europe 9
Egypt 10, 11, 13, 15, 17, 39, 40, 41, 44, 45, 46, 49,
    51, 55, 60, 69, 73, 88, 102, 106, 113, 114, 132,
    144, 145
Essebsi, Béji Caïd 24, 27, 31, 32, 34, 133, 147
Europe 9, 11, 16, 17, 44, 87, 115, 116, 128, 140, 142
European Council 17
European Union 17, 87, 108, 115, 128, 132, 144, 145
Eurozone 118

F
Fatah 15
Fes (Morocco) 59
First World War 12
Fizazi, Mohammed 68
France 9, 11, 12, 16, 17, 19, 20, 24, 25, 89, 95, 100,
    102, 106, 108, 109, 110, 143
    Operation Serval 108, 110, 143
Fukuyama, Francis 137

G
Gadhafi, Muammar 9, 10, 12, 13, 14, 15, 39, 41,
    42, 43, 44, 45, 46, 48, 50, 51, 53, 54, 97, 102, 103,
    104, 105, 106, 107, 108, 110, 111, 132, 133, 134,
    135, 140, 146
Gao (Mali) 95, 100, 107, 108
General Staff Joint-Operations Committee 143
Germany 17
Ghali, Iyad Ag 106, 107
Ghannouchi, Rached 26, 29, 31, 101, 102, 104, 147
Ghardaia (Algeria) 84, 98
Gulf Cooperation Council 118, 143, 144

H
Haftar, Khalifa 40, 41, 44, 46, 48, 49, 50, 51, 55, 144
Hamas 15
Al-Hasiri, Intisar 52
King Hassan II (Morocco) 59, 60, 62
Hejaz 11
Human Rights Watch 51
Husni, Husni Bey 42

I
IMF 36, 67, 90, 118, 119, 120, 122, 123, 125, 139,
    141, 142, 145
In Salah (Algeria) 93
International Institute for Strategic Studies 13
Iran 144
Iraq 33, 41, 89, 98, 99, 110, 111, 136, 139
Islamic Salvation Front 98
Islamic State of Iraq and al-Sham 14, 17, 41, 49, 51,
    53, 54, 55, 89, 94, 98, 106, 110, 111, 139, 140, 144
Israel–Palestine conflict 13

Italy 12, 17, 39
    Operation Triton 17

J
Jaafar, Mustapha Ben 30
Jabhat al-Nusra 89
Japan 16
Jebali, Hamadi 29, 30, 102, 104
Jebel ech Chambi (Tunisia) 94, 105, 142
Jebril, Mahmoud 43, 44, 45, 47
Jeddah (Saudia Arabia) 106, 107
Jomaa, Mehdi 31, 120
Jordan 10, 16, 146
Jund al-Khilafa fi Ard al-Jazair 89

K
Kabylia (Algeria) 99, 101
Kairouan (Tunisia) 104
Keib, Abdurrahman 48
Keïta, Ibrahim Boubacar 110
Kenya 105
Khattala, Ahmed Abu 104
Khost (Afghanistan) 98
Kidal (Mali) 100, 107, 108
Konna (Mali) 108
Kuwait 145

L
Laarayedh, Ali 30, 102, 104
Lagarde, Christine 141
Latin America 9, 100
Leon, Bernardino 42, 52
Levant 11
al-Libi, Abu Anas 102, 105
Libya 9, 10, 11, 12, 13, 14, 15, 16, 17, 18, 33, 39–58,
    60, 73, 87, 88, 89, 94, 97, 98, 101, 102, 103, 105,
    106, 107, 108, 109, 110, 111, 113, 114, 115, 116,
    117, 118, 119, 120, 123, 124, 126, 128, 131, 132,
    133, 134, 135, 137, 138, 139, 141, 142, 143, 144,
    146, 147
    Abu Slim prison 50
    Al-Watan Party 45, 103
    Audit Bureau 119
    Central Bank 47
    Council of State 52
    Cyrenaica 110, 135
    Dawn movement 46, 47, 48, 49, 50, 51, 55, 106, 144
    Dignity movement 40, 46, 50, 106, 144
    Fezzan 135
    General National Congress 44, 45, 47, 48, 103,
        111, 134, 135
    Government of National Accord 17, 52, 135
    House of Representatives 49, 52, 111
    Islamic Legion 107
    Justice and Construction Party 45, 103
    Libyan Islamic Fighting Group 45, 48, 102, 103
    Libyan Revolutionaries Operations Room 48,
        51, 54, 55
    Ministry of Interior 40
        Central Security 40

Mitiga air base 55
Nafusa Mountains 144
National Constituent Assembly 133
National Forces Alliance 45, 47
National Oil Company 47, 115
National Transitional Council 43, 53, 134, 147
National Unity Agreement 17
Nawasi militia 40, 53, 55
Qhaqha militia 48
Rafallah al-Sahati brigades 54
Shura Council of Benghazi Revolutionaries 46
Tripolitania 135
Watan Party 45, 103
Libyan Centre for Strategic and Future Studies 45
London (UK) 17

M
Madani, Ibrahim 50
  Madani militia 48, 50, 53
Maghreb Bank for Investment and Foreign Trade 141
Mali 13, 16, 95, 98, 100, 101, 106, 107, 108, 109, 110, 143
  Ametetai valley 108
  Ansar Eddine 107, 108, 110
  National Movement for the Liberation of Azawad 107
Mansfield, Edward 137
Marzouki, Moncef 121, 140
Mashreq 11, 12
Massoud, Ahmed Shah 101
Mauritania 13, 98, 99, 100, 101, 143
Mediène, Mohamed 'Tewfik' 94
Mediterranean Sea 11, 16, 41, 100
Merghani, Saleh 43, 52, 55
Middle East 9, 10, 11, 12, 14, 16, 17, 99, 110, 113, 122, 132, 137, 140, 144, 145, 148
Misrata (Libya) 43, 44, 46, 47, 48, 49, 50, 51, 54, 111, 144
al-Mitri, Tarek 42
Mohamed, Hamed 48
King Mohammed VI (Morocco) 13, 60, 62, 63, 64, 72, 117, 136
Morocco 9, 10, 11, 13, 14, 15, 16, 18, 59–78, 115, 116, 117, 118, 119, 120, 123, 124, 125, 128, 132, 135, 136, 138, 139, 140, 141, 144, 146
  al-Adl wal-Ihsan 66, 68, 69, 73, 75
  Democratic Way Party 69
  February 20 movement 67, 69, 73, 74
  Istiqlal Party 65
  Justice and Charity movement 66
  Justice and Development Party 63, 65, 66, 67
  Ministry of Islamic Affairs 62
  Moroccan Association of Human Rights 69
  National Human Rights Council 62
  National Initiative for Human Development 62
  Socialist Union of Popular Forces 65
  Unified Socialist Party 69
Morsi, Muhammad 45, 88

Movement for Unity and Jihad in West Africa 95, 100, 107, 108, 109
Mubarak, Hosni 10, 13
Muslim Brotherhood 101, 102, 103, 146
  45, 48, 49, 55

N
NATO 39, 41, 53, 97, 108, 110
New York (US) 104
Niger 109, 110
Nigeria 13
9/11 99, 101, 103
Nobel Peace Prize 31, 147
Norway 16
Nouakchott (Mauritania) 100

O
Obama, Barack 103
OECD 125
Otman-Assed, Ousama 45
Ottoman Empire 11, 20, 39, 40
Ouargla (Algeria) 84
Ouyahia, Ahmed 91

P
Pakistan 102, 109
Paris–Dakar rally 100
Paris (France) 79, 108
Peshawar (Pakistan) 101
Putin, Vladimir 82

Q
Qatar 45, 48, 49, 50, 118, 143, 144, 145

R
River Euphrates 11
River Nile 11
River Tigris 11
Russia 82, 87, 92

S
Sadat, Anwar 92
Sahara 97, 98, 99, 100, 101, 106, 109
Sahel 13
Saleh, Ali Abdullah 10
Sallabi, Ali 48, 50
Saudi Arabia 50, 106, 110, 145
Sellal, Abdelmalek 94
Shoma, Abdullah Salem 40
Siala, Hammouda 47
Sidi Bouzid (Tunisia) 12, 22
Sirte (Libya) 111
el-Sisi, Abdel Fattah 40, 50
Snyder, Jack 137
Soviet Union 98, 101
Spain 17, 74
Statoil (Norway) 16
Stevens, Christopher 42
Sudan 49, 50
Suwaig militia 48

Syria 10, 16, 17, 33, 41, 88, 89, 98, 110, 111, 139, 144, 147
  Free Syrian Army 89

T

Taliban 101, 109
Tanzania 105
Tarhouni, Ali 47
Thinni, Abdullah 43, 48
Timbuktu (Mali) 100, 107, 108
Tobruk (Libya) 47, 49, 51, 106, 111
Touaregs 12, 106, 107, 109, 110
Transparency International 72
Tripoli (Libya) 39, 42, 43, 44, 46, 47, 50, 51, 52, 55, 103, 105, 106, 111
  Fashloum 40
  Green Square 39
  Martyrs' Square 39, 41
  Souk Joumeh 55
Tunisia 9, 10, 11, 12, 14, 15, 17, 18, 19, 19–38, 20, 21, 25, 26, 27, 29, 32, 33, 34, 36, 37, 41, 44, 45, 46, 55, 60, 69, 73, 88, 89, 94, 97, 98, 100, 101, 102, 103, 104, 105, 106, 110, 113, 114, 115, 116, 117, 118, 119, 120, 121, 122, 123, 124, 125, 128, 132, 133, 138, 139, 140, 141, 142, 144, 147
  Afek Tounes 27, 32
  Al Bawsala 29
  Bardo Museum attack 33, 105
  Congress for the Republic 27
  Destour 20, 27
  Ennahda 26, 27, 29, 30, 31, 32, 34, 101, 102, 104, 105, 133, 144, 147
    Shura Council 29
  Ettakatol Party 27
  High Commission for the Fulfilment of the Goals of the Revolution, Political Reform and Democratic Transition 24
  Instance Supérieure Indépendante pour les Élections 25, 31
  Islamic Tunisian Fighting Group 101
  Ministry of Interior 21
  National Constituent Assembly 23, 24, 25, 26, 27, 28, 32, 34
  National Democratic Institute 23, 35
  National Dialogue 30, 31
  Nidaa Tounes 27, 28, 30, 31, 32, 34, 36, 133

Popular Front 30, 31, 32
Progressive Democratic Party 27
Second Republic 102
Sousse attack 17, 34, 106
Truth and Dignity Commission 33
UGTT 30
Union for Tunisia 28
Uqba ibn Nafi Brigade 89, 94
US Embassy attack 29, 104, 140
Tunis (Tunisia) 20, 104, 140
Turkey 49, 101, 132, 144

U

UAE 46, 49, 106, 144, 145
Ukraine 87
United Kingdom 12, 16, 17, 34, 108
United Nations 13, 17, 42, 46, 51, 52, 53, 106, 108, 135, 141, 144, 147
  Support Mission in Libya 52
United States 10, 16, 17, 42, 99, 103, 104, 105, 108, 128, 132, 139, 140, 143, 144, 145
  CIA 105
  National Security Council 10
  State Department 10
  Trade and Investment Framework Agreement 128
  Tunisian-American Enterprise Fund 128

W

Western Sahara 13, 141
Willis, Michael 12
World Bank 71, 114, 123, 124, 125, 126, 138, 141, 142

Y

Yeltsin, Boris 92
Yemen 10, 113, 114, 144
Younes, Abdul-Fattah 43
Yousfi, Youcef 87, 94

Z

al-Zahawi, Muhammad 103
Zawahiri, Ayman 111
Zidane, Ali 43, 48
Zintan (Libya) 43, 46, 48, 50, 54

Adelphi books are published eight times a year by Routledge Journals, an imprint of Taylor & Francis, 4 Park Square, Milton Park, Abingdon, Oxfordshire OX14 4RN, UK.

A subscription to the institution print edition, ISSN 1944-5571, includes free access for any number of concurrent users across a local area network to the online edition, ISSN 1944-558X. Taylor & Francis has a flexible approach to subscriptions enabling us to match individual libraries' requirements. This journal is available via a traditional institutional subscription (either print with free online access, or online-only at a discount) or as part of the Strategic, Defence and Security Studies subject package or Strategic, Defence and Security Studies full text package. For more information on our sales packages please visit www.tandfonline.com/librarians_pricinginfo_journals.

2015 Annual Adelphi Subscription Rates			
Institution	£615	$1,079 USD	€910
Individual	£217	$371 USD	€296
Online only	£538	$944 USD	€796

Dollar rates apply to subscribers outside Europe. Euro rates apply to all subscribers in Europe except the UK and the Republic of Ireland where the pound sterling price applies. All subscriptions are payable in advance and all rates include postage. Journals are sent by air to the USA, Canada, Mexico, India, Japan and Australasia. Subscriptions are entered on an annual basis, i.e. January to December. Payment may be made by sterling cheque, dollar cheque, international money order, National Giro, or credit card (Amex, Visa, Mastercard).

For a complete and up-to-date guide to Taylor & Francis journals and books publishing programmes, and details of advertising in our journals, visit our website: http://www.tandfonline.com.

Ordering information:
USA/Canada: Taylor & Francis Inc., Journals Department, 325 Chestnut Street, 8th Floor, Philadelphia, PA 19106, USA. UK/Europe/Rest of World: Routledge Journals, T&F Customer Services, T&F Informa UK Ltd., Sheepen Place, Colchester, Essex, CO3 3LP, UK.

Advertising enquiries to:
USA/Canada: The Advertising Manager, Taylor & Francis Inc., 325 Chestnut Street, 8th Floor, Philadelphia, PA 19106, USA. Tel: +1 (800) 354 1420. Fax: +1 (215) 625 2940. UK/Europe/Rest of World: The Advertising Manager, Routledge Journals, Taylor & Francis, 4 Park Square, Milton Park, Abingdon, Oxfordshire OX14 4RN, UK. Tel: +44 (0) 20 7017 6000. Fax: +44 (0) 20 7017 6336.

The print edition of this journal is printed on ANSI conforming acid-free paper by Bell & Bain, Glasgow, UK.